"In this riveting treatment of Islam, Daniel Ali skillfully reveals the components of the spiritual war that has raged between the Christian and Muslim worlds. Ali exposes the theological tenets that permanently sanction the use of fear to spread Islam. The fear-induced belief in Allah is something he understands all too well. He describes with complete honesty the Muslims' mandate to defend Islam. Daniel's salvation experience is profound. It is his desire that all who have lived under the oppressive tyranny of Islam are able to live in the freedom and liberty that he now knows. The passion that Daniel lives as a Christian is evident in every aspect of his life. His testimony is valuable to Muslim and Christian alike. It is his hope that Christians will come to understand the obstacles preventing Muslims from listening to the gospel, and that they use this material in their discussions with their Muslim neighbors. *Out of Islam, Free at Last is a must-read for all who seek the Truth.*"

-**Kent Mattox, Word Alive International Outreach, Oxford, Alabama USA**

"In this book, Daniel Ali makes the Muslim mind understandable to westerners. Born in Iraq, brought up Kurdish, he straddles several worlds. Here he makes a case for Jesus Christ, Son of God, possessing Divine Nature, and more, by using verses from the Q'uran.

"*Out of Islam, Free at Last* was written with both the Muslim and Christian audience in mind. He traces his journey out of Islam over years of study in the Qu'ran, the Hadith, the Islamic scholars, as well as the Bible. The Muslim can follow easily, as conflicting Suras and theologies are organized and assembled, very succinctly.

"At the same time, Christians can see and understand perhaps for the first time, the path to walk the Muslim through the Qu'ran that reveals the Son of God. Daniel Ali's vast theological knowledge, coming from years of poring over texts in Arabic, reveals a strategy to confront, challenge and cause to crumble the Islamic monolith."

-**Julia Duin, Religion Editor, The Washington Times**

OUT OF ISLAM
"free at last"

OUT OF ISLAM
"free at last"

DANIEL ALI

TATE PUBLISHING & *Enterprises*

 Tate Publishing
& Enterprises

Out of Islam
Copyright © 2007 by Daniel Ali. All rights reserved.
Visit www.tatepublishing.com for more information.

No part of this publication may be reproduced, stored in a retrieval system or transmitted in any way by any means, electronic, mechanical, photocopy, recording or otherwise without the prior permission of the author except as provided by USA copyright law.

Scripture quotations marked "NIV" are taken from the *Holy Bible, New International Version*®, Copyright © 1973, 1978, 1984 by International Bible Society. Used by permission of Zondervan Publishing House. All rights reserved.

Koran quotations are from The Holy Qur'an, Abdullah Yusuf Ali, 10th Edition, English and Arabic, 1997. Amana Publications, Beltsville, Maryland.

The opinions expressed by the author are not necessarily those of Tate Publishing, LLC.

This book is designed to provide accurate and authoritative information with regard to the subject matter covered. This information is given with the understanding that neither the author nor Tate Publishing, LLC is engaged in rendering legal, professional advice. Since the details of your situation are fact dependent, you should additionally seek the services of a competent professional.

Book design copyright © 2007 by Tate Publishing, LLC. All rights reserved.
Cover design by Sommer Buss
Interior design by Lindsay B. Behrens

Published in the United States of America

ISBN: 1-5988676-1-X
07.05.18

TO THE LATE DOC BLEVINS, WHO HUMBLY ASKED
ME TO PRAY WITH HIM, AND WHO BROUGHT ME
TO THE LORD, SEPTEMBER 17, 1995.

FOREWORD

I have had the privilege of knowing the author and seeing his passion to reach his people with the gospel message. His second book *Out of Islam, Free at Last* is the history of God's Grace that changed his heart and mind.

Centuries ago, Paul wrote, "For I am not ashamed of the gospel of Christ, for it is the power of God to salvation for everyone who believes, for the Jew first and also for the Greek" (Romans 1:16 NKJV). In *Out of Islam, Free at Last*, Daniel answers and obeys the command of Jesus, "Go home to your friends, and tell them what great things the Lord has done for you, and how He has had compassion on you" (Mark 5:19 NKJV).

It is a joy to see Muslims turning their hearts to Jehovah God, the True and Living God of the Bible. As a result, the message changed their lives and affected their intellect, emotions and will. Adherents to the gospel, they are willing to suffer persecution, and to pay the ultimate sacrifice for their faith. Their boldness, courage, perseverance, and even their blood, form the seeds that will plant and nourish many underground churches.

A Christian endures not to EARN the favor of God, since that favor was won for us, if we accept it, in Jesus' death on the cross. The offering of the believer's life is made in response and appreciation to the One Who loved him first, until death.

Islam is a threat to Christianity, while at the same time it is a great challenge. Islam and Christianity are mutually exclusive; both cannot be the Truth. The core of Islamic teaching denies every fundamental doctrine taught in the Bible. Islam rejects the crucifixion, the Trinity and the God of the Bible. It denies that Jesus is the Son of God, that He died on the cross, was raised from the dead and ascended into Heaven in His resurrected body. Islam asserts there is no original sin, and, as such, there is no need for a savior's atonement. Islam does not offer its followers of the assurance of eternal life, as it rejects God's forgiveness through Jesus Christ.

Islam presents to the church a challenge. Our lives are at risk in Islamic countries when we evangelize. But the Christian is told to go into the uttermost parts of the world, to reach them in our communities, and across the globe with the message of hope, reconciliation to God, and His gift of eternal life. Our Lord stated that people from all nations would be gathered around the throne in the kingdom of God including Muslims. "They will come from the east and the west, from the north and the south, and sit down in the kingdom of God" (Luke 13:29 NKJV).

Reaching Muslims has often been the most difficult of tasks. *Out of Islam, Free at Last* is an invaluable aid in obeying Jesus' command to witness to our Muslim neighbor. The encouraging news is that after the September 11, 2001 attacks, the Church entered a new era of opportunity. Signs of a breakthrough are clearly visible, and signs of progress have abounded. In Iran, the Middle East and North Africa, the numbers of Christians from Muslim backgrounds has multiplied. In Morocco and Algeria, Church growth has been impressive, especially among the Berber peoples. Even in Iran, the number of believers has doubled in the last three years.

God is intent upon opening the eyes of tens of thousands of Muslims. He is preparing His church for a great harvest, and there is no doubt many will come from Islam to salvation in Jesus Christ. Jesus proclaimed, "I am the way, the truth, and the life. No one comes to the Father except through Me" (John 14:6 NKJV).

Pastor Tony Ghareeb
Arabic Bible Baptist Church
Fairfax Station , Virginia USA

Table of Contents

CHILDHOOD 19
ORIGINAL SIN 27
CREATED IN THE IMAGE OF GOD 39
PEACEFUL ISLAM 41
RADICAL ISLAM 49
THE WARS WITH THE JEWS 67
THE SON OF PROMISE: ISAAC OR ISHMAEL? 75
PROPHETS IN ISLAM 81
THE ISLAMIC CLAIM THAT THE BIBLE IS CORRUPTED . . . 91
MUSLIMS' CONFUSION ABOUT THE HOLY SPIRIT 109
CHRISTIAN CULTS ON JESUS CHRIST 113
JESUS WAS NOT LIKE ADAM 115
THE DIVINE NATURE OF JESUS CHRIST 117
ARE GOD AND ALLAH ONE AND THE SAME? 127
GROWING UP UNDER SADDAM HUSSEIN 135
NEW COUNTRY, NEW LIFE AND NEW FAITH 139
FROM ISLAM TO THE FLOCK OF JESUS CHRIST 145
EVANGELISM: THE CROWNS AT HIS FEET 151
ENDNOTES 153

INTRODUCTION

What must happen for a devout Muslim to convert from Islam to Christianity? Muslims erroneously believe that no Muslim in his right mind would forsake the one true religion of Allah. Muslims believe to forsake Islam is to commit one of the three most reprehensible sins: the most detestable of all, apostasy. "Lo! Those who disbelieve after their profession of belief, and afterward grow in infidelity, their repentance will never be accepted. And such are those who are astray" (Koran 3:90).

If one declares a faith other than his native Islam, he faces death at the hands of any Muslim who discovers him. At the very least, he or she becomes totally outcast from society. The isolation confronts him at every turn. Because Islam provides a complete legal structure, court system, school system, and Islam governs relationships in business, culture, and the family, a convert to another faith suffers unique consequences for leaving Islam. Jewish families are known to sever all ties and actually hold funerals for their children who convert to Christianity. Similarly, the Muslims feel horror, shame, and a belief that that the convert has "become an apostate worthy of death."

In the West, we have become accustomed to thinking of our elder years with such safeguards as Medicaid and Social Security when we are too old to work. The social network provided in Islamic cultures IS ONLY the family. There IS no provision for those who shame their families and are cast out of their families. In America, if our situation became grave, we could as a last resort, rely on the good graces of strangers, and still never go hungry. However, if one is ostracized and cast out by his Muslim family, no one else will have pity on him or her. In fact, Muslims believe that your death would be a good lesson for others as to what happens when one shames his family.

In Western Christian culture, one's unique identity is valued; his talents will take him a long way toward self-sufficient and independent living. We consider it a necessity for young people to support themselves, and to live independent of their parents. This simply is not the culture of a Muslim family.

A Muslim young person does not think of moving away from the family to establish his or her own identity. Rather, their identity comes from being part of the family, and the tribe. The family's reputation will accompany the individual wherever he goes. The tribe and the region determine much of the Muslim's financial and educational opportunities; his employment will come through that line, as well as his, or her, future marriage partner. The individual's responsibility is to improve and better his family and tribe. His security in life depends on his family.

Muslim society is said to be a brotherhood; thus, to betray or shame your own family is to betray the whole of Islamic society. The Muslim conscience is formed from a very early age. Your Muslim conscience will never take you an opposite direction from your parents' will. No Muslim will defend you, nor will anyone support you should you claim that you "followed your conscience" in choosing a faith other than Islam.

The purpose of your conscience is not to express your individuality, but to guarantee your collective identity survives. Your conscience is there to further the good name of the whole family. It is there to keep you in obligation to your family, as well as to defend Islam. These powerful views of self and my family had to be broken before I could look to what other faiths offered. I needed something to further split the pottery of my life so that truthful beams of light might come through the cracks.

Islam itself has many cracks through which light can come, but one difficulty is that most Muslims never bother to study their faith. The further they study, the less answer they have, and this is an uncomfortable place for any Muslim to be. It is not wise to discuss openly your doubts about Islam. But the Lord promises that if we seek Him, He *WILL BE* found. May the glory be God's that He did not leave me in darkness but chose to bring me into His beautiful light!

Although I have waited ten years to put to paper just how the Lord Jesus Christ saved me from eternal damnation, I have come to believe that my testimony might be valuable for both Christians and Muslims to read. It may bear some light for the Christian wanting to answer the questions Muslims pose before leaving Islam.

I faced the impossibility of remaining a Muslim once I tackled the theological contradictions in the Koran with an honest heart. I found that the Lord bore witness to Himself in the Koran, but that this witness is hidden to those who refuse to seek, knock, and ask. In the pages of the Koran, we read the Truth of the Trinity, Who Jesus Christ is, and Who God is, never opening a Bible. The Koran, held as sacred by the Muslim, can actually be his path to accepting Jesus Christ as his Lord and Savior. Our task is to provide the sparks in the Koran that will lead those who are called to the truth.

Conversions come not as result of persuasive debate, but rather from the passion of the Holy Spirit. For centuries, gentiles and Jews converted without the use of a written Bible, but rather by the spoken Word, mixed with faith and love. This remains possible today. As well, we need to know when to "shake the dust off our feet and walk away."

CHILDHOOD

I remember clearly, one day, my brothers set off to see a movie in the only cinema in my birthplace in Iraq. I cried so hard, kicking my legs in the dusty road, screaming that they should take me. My shed tears, by hook or by crook, stimulated the heart of my elder brother, who came back to bring me along to the movie theater. There are only a few clips of the movie that I still remember. One of these was that a mother, with tears in her eyes, placed her infant child in a basket and released it down the river. Down the stream was a group of young women playing along the banks of the river; one of them saw the basket floating nearby and, to her astonishment, a child was lying in the basket.

"He must be a Hebrew child!" shouted the princess, who took the baby as hers. The child grew to become a young man, and his name was Moses. I am sure that the miracles in the movie imprinted on my young mind the glorious deeds of an almighty God.

I remember the very first day I went to school. Our teacher asked us to repeat after him, "Al Islamu denana wa Muhammad rasulana." This translates to English as "Islam is our religion and Muhammad is our prophet [messenger]." These were the words to a song we learned later on in the first grade, even before we could read or write. Someone once said, "Teaching a child is like writing on a rock." Muslims believe in early instruction in Islam as though it engraves the future. There is no separation of religion from education in the Middle East.

My dad used to take us, the boys, to a Huseineyya (a Shiite Mosque) during the annual anniversary of Imam Hussein's martyrdom. Hussein was one of the sons of Ali, Muhammad's cousin, a great hero and highly venerated figure for Shiite Muslims.

The Imam of the Mosque prophesied to my dad that one of my brothers and I would become very religious in the future, though he did not like me much. Occasionally I would ask this Imam questions which he did not like. I look back in wonder now as to what questions I asked that so irritated him. The prophecy was right in that both my brother and I sought God, but this same brother remains a Muslim, and I now have come to the light of Jesus Christ. We do have our brotherly discussions about Jesus; he is coming along, and it is just a matter of time for him to convert.

We lived close to a railroad station during the 1960s in Iraq. Once in awhile, there came nearby many political prisoners, Kurdish freedom fighters and communists. At times they were handcuffed, and some ran away. Oh, how I loved the ones who ran away! Growing up as a Kurd in Saddam's nightmare was not easy for me or for others. My heroes became those who broke the mold, those who were brave and those who were martyred.

I was taught to observe the tenants of Islam; prayers in any language other than Arabic were "not heard" by Allah. The Koran was delivered in Arabic, the language of Heaven. I told my mother one day, when I was old enough to verbalize it, that I would pray in Kurdish, my own language. She reprimanded me: "Prayers should be in Arabic, since Muhammad prayed and commanded our prayers to be in Arabic only." "A child can speak two languages, so why doesn't Allah understand Kurdish?" Mom did not like my assertive questions, but Dad smiled when he had to rebuke me for thinking that way.

My next-door neighbors were Chaldean Catholics, and yet I had no way to know what Christianity meant! Christians were forbidden from evangelizing, and thus said little.

I knew their names were neither Arab nor Kurdish, but, oh, they were kind and gentle. Most important to me was that their mother always gave me candy.

That candy and kindness was enough for me to love them then, but now I love them for the many other ways they bore witness to me. I saw sadness in them and a reluctance to be at ease, and I wondered why they felt this way. Now I realize they felt sadness because they loved me and knew that I was missing Jesus by growing up as a Muslim child.

It is customary among Muslims not to use dishes, knives, or any appliances used by Christians, since Muslims believe that Christians are unclean because they eat pork. Our Christian neighbor borrowed a sharp knife from us to cut a large piece of meat. We lent the knife to them, but my father automatically assumed they would use it to cut pork. When they returned the knife, and my grandfather asked my mother to wash the knife before using it, Mom said no.

My mother replied, out of custom, in a very Kurdish way. She said, "If the Name of God,

most merciful, and most compassionate, would not clean the knife, no water in the world would. Our neighbors are decent and loving people, and I do not believe that they are Kufar."

(This term is the plural of Kafir, which means "unbeliever.")

I admired Mom for her answer of faith in God, and for her wit. To this day, I search between the lines of what she says and does for her innate wisdom. I had a similar feeling towards John Doe, my little Christian friend and primary school classmate. I did not accept that he was an unbeliever. His character stood out from the rest and bore witness to me.

John Doe was meek and humble and very peaceful. Other kids once teased him about his faith. I beat those kids so hard that afterwards I was called "the friend of Christians." It was derogatory, at best. Many abuses showered on Christians fell on me as well. These abuses I shall not add

to my resume here on earth, but I am sure the Merciful Lord took note of them all.

The northern Iraqi town where I grew up was divided among Sunnis and Shiites, which was uncharacteristic; Saddam had Arabized the north, and most of it had become Sunni. Another unusual occurrence in my childhood was that, though there were some Christians in the towns we moved to, we invariably had Christians as next-door neighbors. Either they were Chaldean Catholics, or they were Assyrian Christians.

The Eastern Christian sects had some animosity among them, which was evident for an outsider like me, then a Muslim. My neighbor's son always had black clothes on. I did not know then that he was a priest, but I will never forget him. In later years, he gave me a book titled "Christian Martyrs," which was the first glimpse I had of the faith. What a beautiful example was set for me in my youth! I read and admired all of the

Christian martyrs, whose examples were total contrast to the martyrs of my religion, Islam.

The former were martyred without killing others, enduring torture without denying Christ, and they died having shed no innocent blood. But the "martyrs" of Islam were warriors who died while shedding the blood of others, the non-Muslims.

The Christian priest once told me when I was tempted to punch his little brother, "A strong man forgives the weak person, and only weak people cannot forgive." These words seemed eternal, powerful and in vibrant contrast to my faith! "Forgive your enemies" was destiny coming from the mouth of that wonderful and gentle priest. I thought it was his phrase, as I did not know from whom these words truly came. God's Word does not return to Him void.

The ancient name for the Kurds is the Medes. The Kurds have an important destiny in Scripture. The Medes are the only ancient people group about whom no negative prophecy was given in the Bible. God refers to the Medes as His warriors whom He has preserved until the Last Days to be called out from the mountains to defeat His enemies.

Daniel, the Jewish prophet, was taken captive to Babylon. Daniel came eventually to serve under Darius, the Mede, who was king during the Mede-Persian Empire, which overtook Babylon. It was King Darius, the Mede, who was forced to throw Daniel to the lions. It was Darius, the Mede, who ran to the lions' den at dawn, crying out, "Did your God save you?" The king was overjoyed and filled with faith in the God of Israel as a result. He decreed that all of the empire would worship the God of the Jews. He installed Daniel as consultant to His Majesty, and the Medes were privy to Daniel's prophecies about the coming Messiah. Some we find in the book of Daniel in Scripture; others are recorded in the annals of the Medes.

In fact, much of the ancient Zoroastrian religion of the Medes (Kurds) came directly from the prophet Daniel while he was in Babylon. We find the ancient language of the Kurds in the stone tablets of the Zoroastrians. Daniel's prophecy to the Medes was that the coming Messiah would be born under the sign of a miraculous star. The wise men (Maji) who brought gifts to the baby Jesus were Medes (Kurds) who were tribal designates.

These "three wise men" were the FIRST Gentiles to worship Christ, yet the Kurds remain today the *last and largest population still unreached* with the Gospel. They were the first to come, but apparently they are among the last to receive the full Gospel. To date, the Scripture has not been fully translated into the two main Kurdish dialects for tens of millions to read, though *it has been translated by Wycliffe for people groups as small as 500.*

Daniel's prophecies stated that the Messiah would come and reign as a priest and King, and this Messiah would die and shed His blood for the remission of sins for all mankind. Thus, the "three wise men" brought gifts of gold for the newborn King, frankincense for His office as priest, and the embalming myrrh for His death.

Zoroastrians are mistakenly said to be fire worshippers. Fires are still lit on the mountainsides on Newroz, the New Year, on March 21. Fire is a symbol of the purifying fire of God's Spirit, and it is in no way an object of worship. The Zoroastrians are also mistakenly said to be astrologers, but they watched the heavens for the sign of the miraculous birth, not for astrological readings. Because they watched and waited, God rewarded them with the honor of being at His bedside. That is how they came to the cradle of Jesus; they believed that God's Prophecy through Daniel would be fulfilled.

Muslims celebrate Newroz (New Year) across Afghanistan, Iran, Iraq, Turkey, and elsewhere in the Middle East, without those populations realizing that it came from the Zoroastrians, from the very time Daniel was delivering his prophecies about the coming Messiah to the Gentiles. Iranians and others like to claim that Zarathustra was their own native son. However, to this day, Daniel's remains lie buried in Kurdistan of Iraq, and his grave is honored there still.

Kurds throughout history have helped the Jews when they were captive in Babylon, and Kurds have remained a friend to the Jews up to today. The Arabs hate the Kurds for that. In fact, the Kurds are often called the second Jews of the Middle East, as though it were a bad name! However, in Scripture we find a great love God has for the Kurds. He praises them, saying, "They can neither be bought with gold or silver." See Isaiah 13:17. Truly, the Kurds remain His to the end of time. May Christian evangelists everywhere see the harvest is wide open and waiting to be reaped.

My classmate John Doe was always asked to leave the class when the subject was Islam.

I could not understand why should he leave if we were eager to win him to Islam?

When I asked why we treated the unbelievers differently, my teacher answered me that they have chosen not to follow Islam on purpose, since it is the real nature of all human beings to be Muslims, as Muhammad said, and the Koran confirms. Thus, Muslims teach their young to discriminate against unbelievers ad infinitum. This bothered my conscience deeply.

Even worse, the Koran states that sometimes Allah *CHOOSES TO LEAD* people into perdition.

What sort of God could willfully lead people to eternal death? All of this bothered my childhood conscience. We cannot find the expressed love of Allah in the Koran. We find instead an anthropomorphic view of Allah, though Muhammad intended otherwise. Allah is said by Muhammad to have some of the same intolerance and unloving ways as man.

If Allah is so far above humans, he should be far above in love, as well. He must surpass the good character of which we know mankind is capable. He created humans and thus must have a purpose in so doing. Yet the Koran says that Allah purposely created some humans for eternal damnation and for a bad example to the only ones he loves, the Muslims. I loved my Christian neighbors; so did Allah not love them? Why would Allah create such good people as the Christians I knew if he only destined them for hell? I was troubled by such contradictions and found no one could address them, other than to quote the Koran again.

Islam requires that all Muslims see themselves as a brotherhood. This has serious implications for how Muslims are to treat and take care of one another. It is this majestic sense of worldwide brotherhood that pilgrims feel they experience on the Hajj to Mecca.

This brotherhood of Muslims, or Umma, or community, is to be a tight-knit bond between *ALL* Muslims. Yet when it came to the Kurds, *NOT ONE MUSLIM COUNTRY SPOKE UP.* We were persecuted, slaughtered by other Muslims, and bombed with chemical weapons, but not one cry from a Muslim "brother" was heard. In fact, not one single country objected when Saddam threw chemical weapons on us. We experienced the hatred that the Jews have endured for centuries. We know what it is to be slain as lambs, and I am proud of the Kurdish heritage and character given us by God, which has formed us and made us ready to receive Christ.

Muslims give a lot of lip service to the phrase," We are all brothers. If one suffers, the rest will, too." *I could never understand the reason for the Arab nations' inaction and deafening silence.* Perhaps it is because Arabs consider themselves to be the only true Muslims. Perhaps it is such arrogance that leaves the suffering of Indonesian Muslim victims of the 2004 tsunami unanswered by most wealthy Arab nations. Or, I could refer to the suffering of Pakistanis and Iranians and Turks in their earthquakes. Let me neither overlook the suffering of many starving African Muslims. It is the Christian nations that give aid and comfort to the suffering around the world, because only a Christian sees the real brotherhood of mankind as created in God's Image.

Muslims do not believe that people are created in God's Image. The power of the belief that men are created in the Image of God cannot be overstated.

The Islamic world in general, and Arabs most importantly, did *nothing* to condemn or speak out against Saddam for massacring the Kurds. On the contrary, many countries around the world profited from the oil Saddam took from the Kurds, and they hoped for the demise of the Kurds once and for all. Yet the Kurds, through holocaust and war, century after century, have risen again from the ashes. God tells us, through Isaiah and Jeremiah, that *He Himself* has preserved the Kurds until the End Times. *May God be proved true and every man a liar.*

However, simply being persecuted by your "brethren" is not sufficient to make one doubt his faith. Because others betray him and move about like Judas, the man of faith might become stronger, not always weaker. The Muslims cannot say that I became a believer in Jesus Christ because I was persecuted, beaten, condemned to death by Saddam, or abandoned by others. No man was able to stop the Lord from taking over my life, and no man is able to stop the salvation that God has ordained for the Kurds.

As Muslims betrayed their Muslim brothers in direct disobedience to the words and dictates of the Koran itself, I remained determined to study, not just blindly follow Islam. I embarked on a years' long, systematic and careful study of the Koran. I am thrilled that the Lord honored my seeking, knocking and asking.

When I did not understand specific doctrines, I would refer to other sources, sometimes asking my religion teacher about them. It was mandatory for every grade in school to teach religion

Never did I find the truth until I read the pages of the Holy Bible. And nothing has unlocked the mysteries of God and His surpassing love as has the Bible, which the Holy Spirit inspired.

I did not hate the Arabs as I grew up; I simply thought they did not know any better and that they were stubbornly ignorant. To the contrary, I have many more reasons to love them since the Lord Jesus Christ paid for their sins as well, and He loved them enough to endure the Cross for them. Need I say more? Arabs are among those created in God's Image and likeness, and I dare not hate God's Image in my fellow human beings.

ORIGINAL SIN

In this written testimony, I will explore and expose in depth the tenets of Islam that drove me from the religion. These are powerful keys to sharing the Christian faith with a Muslim.

There are doctrines in the Koran that deserve our scrutiny. I begin with Adam's sin, or what we call "original sin." The Muslim view of original sin is crucial for Christians to understand if we are to find ourselves effective when sharing our faith. Unless the hearer is convinced he carries within himself original sin, he will see no need for Jesus

First, Muslims agree that Adam and Eve sinned, but they claim Allah forgave them of this sin immediately. There was no original sin, from Adam, that was passed down from one generation to the next. Each person has to account *only* for his own personal sin. So, we see that original sin needs our immediate attention and resolution. For Jesus' blood to apply, the person must first be convinced that there is something for which he cannot make restitution. We will discuss this fully.

Second, I wish to expose here, briefly, the sinister claim made by all Muslims: that the Bible as we know it is *not* the original Word of God... that this Bible was conveniently altered by early followers of Jesus, and that Muhammad's name and prophecies concerning his coming were deleted. Muslims are forbidden, in general, to read a Bible. Yet many have a curiosity about it.

I will examine Muslims' claim that the Bible was altered or corrupted.

Thirdly, it is important for the Christian to realize that Muslims *do not* believe the promise of God came through Abraham's son, Isaac. They believe, rather, that Abraham's first son, Ishmael, born of Sarah's Egyptian handmaid, was the son of the Promise, and that it was Ishmael who was sacrificed by Abraham. This effectively deletes the Jews from being the people of God, and places the Arabs as the chosen people of Allah all along. We will look at this claim as well.

The concept of original sin is basically *absent* in Islamic theology, as we stated before.

It is considered the first forgiven sin and that is the end of the matter, yet the Koran barely provides any support for such claim. In fact, the evidence for original sin passed down from Adam is more abundant in the Koran.

Disputes over the concept of original sin did not originate with the advent of Islam. In the fifth century, some religious heresies denied the concept of original sin, saying that the sin of Adam harmed Adam alone and had no consequences or effect on the human race. Throughout the first six centuries after Jesus' death and resurrection, intense theological debates occurred, causing innumerable sects and divisions. The Catholic Church hoped to unite the faithful by determining true doctrine via international councils. Out of these councils came such pronouncements as the Nicene Creed, the doctrines of the Holy Trinity, and the Divine and Human Natures of Christ, to name a few. As far back as St. Paul's day, it was necessary to contend for the faith, as he records, "The cross is foolishness to the Gentiles and scandal to the Jews."

There are striking similarities between Muhammad's view of Adam's sin and prior Christian heresies. Muhammad had occasion to debate with Christians who had fled to the desert to avoid persecution by the Catholic Church. Since he was illiterate, he learned only the doctrines he heard from Christian cults. He was unaware these Christians were not main-stream.

Some of the prevailing heresies are summarized by Saint Augustine in his book, "Confessions."

> That Adam was made mortal, and that he would have died, whether he sinned or did not sin; that Adam's sin injured himself alone, and not the human race; that the law, no less than the Gospel leads us to the kingdom; that before the coming of Christ there were persons without sin; that newborn infants are in the same condition that Adam was before the transgression; that, on the one hand, the entire human race does not die on account of Adam's death and transgression; nor, on the other hand, does the whole human race rise again through the resurrection of Christ . . . [1]

The denial of original sin is not the only doctrinal similarity that Islam has with sixth-century heresies in the region. Muhammad's view of Jesus Christ—His person, mission, and nature—is in agreement with the Judaizers who held similar beliefs about Jesus; that He was no more than a mere man, etc.

One of the most striking differences between the ancient heresies and Islam is that the latter carries within its own theology, the Koran and Muhammad's Tradition, *both* sides of the debates. The Muslim's view that no original sin was passed down from Adam comes from the fact that it is not mentioned by name either in the Koran or in Muhammad's Tradition. Yet, we clearly see there is original sin both in compelling and implicit texts!

Since mankind is created in the Image of God, the Bible indicates *all* sin is sin against God. However, our fellow man suffers from our sins, as well. Do we find these claims about sin in Islam? In general, Muslims say that if you sin, you sin against yourself. There are only a few sins that are directly against Allah. Thus, we see huge emphasis on them . . . sins such as blasphemy, idol worship, and the like.

In Islam, one of the three unforgivable sins is called *shirk*, or idol worship. Idol worship is any form of worship given to something other than Allah (such as to Jesus Christ) or believing that God had some partner, such as a Son or the Holy Spirit. We ask why *shirk*, or idol worship, in Islam, is of such gravity that it cannot be forgiven.

The answer is two fold. The first is because Allah declared it so,[2] and the second is that, in worshiping any other object(s) as equal to or associated with Allah, humans diminish the only worthy object of their worship, Allah. These declarations in the Koran were directed at Jesus and the Holy Spirit, and they betray Muhammad's effort to discredit the Trinity. "There is no god but Allah, and Muhammad is his messenger" is the archetype of faith for the Muslim.

The sins against Allah, such as *shirk* are unforgivable in Islam, and are of infinite gravity since they offend the one infinite being, Allah! Let us keep this point in mind; later in this chapter we will be dealing with the issue again. In Christianity, sin against an infinite God has infinite magnitude, and thus sins' remission *cannot* come from a finite being.

Muslim scholars attest that men's sins have affected all of creation. "Mischief has appeared on the land and the sea on account of what the hands of men have earned; that He may give them a taste of some of [the actions] they have done, in order that they may return."[3] This mischief, flung upon all of creation, occurred, according to the Koran, as the result of "the sins of men!"

Hence the relationship between human sin and the chaos of the world is affirmed in the Koran!

Allah is NOT to blame for man's sins, so it is certainly Adam's sin, and all mankind since, which must have affected the whole creation. We know that Islam does not hold Allah responsible for man's sins, but rather Adam himself, since Adam was not in the state of chaos when God created him, and his dwelling place was Paradise.

The Koran is clear in this passage that man's sins *have* affected all of creation, yet Muslims vehemently deny this as Christian false ideology. At the core of the issue is whether or not original sin can be transmitted. Muslims agree with Christians that sin is first and foremost an offense against God; and that some of these sins are deadly or unforgivable, and that other sins are forgivable. However, they completely disagree with Christians on how sin is resolved, i.e., as to whether or not man can redeem himself from a state of sin and its consequent effects.

Muslims believe that all humans on Judgment Day will stand before the throne of God to be judged according to the weight of their deeds. The weight of these deeds will be balanced as a scale. One side is for the good deeds and the other for the evil deeds. If the scale tips towards the evil deeds, the person will be doomed to hell fire (Koran 7:8–9); otherwise he will be in Paradise, enjoying the company of seventy-two ever-virgin maids who remain virgins no matter how many times he sleeps with them. Every conceivable carnal desire[4] he has shall be fulfilled, even with young boys[5], as a reward for his being a faithful Muslim on earth.

There is no clear claim that non-Muslims can enter this Paradise. Their deeds and faith determine their entry into Paradise. Islam is humanistic, works-based moral ideology. Muhammad said,

"In the judgment day, Allah will present to every Muslim a Jew or Christian as a ransom to be killed, if the Muslim wants to avoid hell fire."[6]

So, the Muslims *DO* have the notion of a ransom. Here Islam holds that the ransom for their sins is for them to kill a Jew or a Christian.

Any Christian or Jew who heard about the Koran and Muhammad, but chose to remain in his previous faith, would go to hell. "In whom Muhammad's soul is in his hand, any Christians or Jews who hear about me and die without believing in that which I was sent with [Koran] he will be of the people of the hell fire."[7] According to the Koran, all non-believers in Islam go to hell.

Humanism replaces the need for God's grace with the works and potential of man. Man should be able to achieve good works, attain noble goals, and redeem himself. Man is at the center of his own destiny, not God. It is fair to say that Islam's claims and Muslims' thinking follow humanistic tendencies more often than not. The Koran teaches that Muslims can redeem themselves with good deeds, eliminating any need for Jesus as Redeemer or Savior.

Not only do Muslims refute the Sonship of Jesus Christ and His saving blood, but they deny that He died at all. A majority believe Jesus died, but not on the cross. They say Allah caused Jesus to die and raised Him up to Himself. It was inconceivable to Muhammad that God would allow His special Holy one to die such a horrible death in crucifixion. The Koran claims that Allah substituted a Jesus look-alike on the cross, and let that person deceive the faithful and die a horrible death instead of Jesus.

Yet the mystery of God's love is that He sent His *only* innocent Son to take our place upon the cross, that whosoever would accept this remission, would be redeemed from his sins and be saved.

It truly is a revelation of extreme and extravagant *LOVE* that we read in the Bible. We do not find this extravagant love anywhere else but in God the Father, expressly revealed in God, the Son, Who willingly went in our place, enduring the shame and punishment for our sins on our behalf.

We see in the Bible a Holy God Who sacrifices His only Son, Jesus, in our place.... this was foreshadowed when Abraham offered up his only son in an act of faith. See Genesis 22:16. Muslims know that Abraham, a mere man, was capable of such noble character, but they cannot attribute even this human level to Allah. Muhammad somehow missed the beautiful heart of the loving Father. He knew that God's ways are far above our ways, but Muhammad often attributed human traits to Allah without realizing he had done so.

Islam claims that Allah is transcendent, and thus man will never be able to have fellowship with Allah. The utter "otherness" of Allah means He remains unknowable, even in Paradise. Yet the Koran actually ascribes qualities and shortcomings to Allah that even Abraham surpassed when he offered up his son. Allah is unknowable and transcendent, but according to the Koran, he is also capable, apparently, of character less than Abraham.

I ask here, did men, with limited knowledge of Christianity, write the Koran? It is difficult to convince a Muslim, for example, that the Koran makes false claims about Christianity. Muslims are forbidden to open a Bible. They avoid reading it by saying the Bible was corrupted and altered by earlier believers to exclude the prophecies about Muhammad. But also, the Muslims do not read the Koran analytically or contextually, and thus they miss the inconsistencies and contradictions therein.

Man himself could never have conceived of such surpassing love unless God Himself had revealed it. This mysterious love has been the inspiration of all the Christian martyrs who willingly went to their deaths with joy rather than betray the one who gave all for us.

Once Muhammad rejected the notion of original sin, he was forced to reject salvation through Jesus Christ. Original sin was such an abhorrent thought because man would then have a problem he himself could not solve.

Muhammad could not accept that man was created in the Image of God. This sounded like a blasphemy to Muhammad. Somehow, he thought Allah would never have created man in his own Image and Likeness. Man and Allah, human and Divine, shall never meet, even in the next life.

Muhammad claimed the sin of Adam was "the first forgiven sin": and that Adam's sin was his personal sin alone. He was then forced to deny that Adam's sin had any effect at all on others, even upon his offspring, Cain and Able. Adam's sin had a singular, personal dimension only, according to the Muslims. But the Christian sees all sin as having both individual and collective dimensions! When we sin, we affect our own relationship with God, but we also affect the entire Body of Christ.

How do we prove to Muslims that Adam's sin was transmitted? We find the *other* sources in the Koran that provide evidence for original sin.

Both sides of most theological debates are covered in the Koran, so let us proceed to the other crucial claims of Muhammad. We begin to see the contradictions the Muslim has to accommodate in his religion.

Allah created Adam from dust and clay (Koran 15:26); with his spirit [Allah's], he gave Adam life. The Muslim version of Adam does not show Allah allowing Adam to name the animals as we read in Genesis 2:19. Rather, in the Koran, Allah taught Adam the names for the animals, since the angelic beings had failed to do so! The angels protested to Allah, claiming,

"How could we name them if thou hast not taught us?" and he taught Adam the names of everything, then he showed them to the angels and said, "Tell me the names of these if you are truthful." They said, "Glory be to you, we have no knowledge except what you have taught us, only you are the all wise." He said, "O, Adam, inform them with their names."[8]

In Islam, the purpose for which Allah has created Adam was for Adam to be his "vicegerent," or agent, on earth. The Arabic term used to express this position is Khalefa (Caliph), which can also mean "successor" (Koran 2:30). To our amazement, these same angelic beings had foreknowledge that this "successor" would shed blood upon the earth, so they questioned Allah's wisdom in creating a vicegerent on earth. Allah responded, "They knew not what he knew."[9]

Allah is in charge of all that is in heaven and on earth; by creating Adam (thus all mankind) to be his vicegerent or agent on earth, mankind was given a mission to care for this earth. The Biblical comparison for Muhammad's assertion is God's command that Adam have dominion over the earth. We have not fulfilled this position of trust and care due to original sin.

The stain of original sin is so prevalent in our lives that not only are we poor caretakers, but we remain incapable of subduing the earth. In reality, it is we who are subdued by the earth and its power.

God provided everything necessary to abundant life on earth, and all of Adam's needs were met in the Garden of Eden. Only one thing was forbidden to Adam: to eat from the tree of knowledge of good and evil. This was distinct from the Tree of Life. God set the boundaries for Adam and Eve within which His presence would be known, and Adam and Eve's provision therein would be abundant.

In the Koran, the Garden is located in Paradise (Jena').

> Satan says to them, "Your lord has not forbidden you to eat of this tree, for he knows that when you eat from it, you shall be like the angels and live for eternity." And he swore to them that he was sincere in his advice. By deception he brought them to the tree; when they tasted the tree, their shame became apparent to them, and they began covering themselves with the leaves of the tree. Their lord called out to them, saying, "Did I not forbid you not to eat from the tree and told you that Satan is your enemy?"[10]

The text above implies the fall of Satan, since he disobeyed the commands of Allah to "bow down to Adam." The Koran claims that Allah commanded the angels to bow down to Adam, but some refused and thus disobeyed. "'Why have you not bowed down to the one I have created with my hands?' he said. But the fallen angel justified himself, 'I am better than he; you have created me from fire, while you have created him [Adam] from clay.'"[11]

Satan (Iblis in Arabic) tempted Adam and Eve (Hawa') to eat from the tree, and so they did.

> But Satan whispered to him, "O, Adam! Shall I show thee the Tree of Immortality, and a possession that wasteth not away?" Then the two of them [Adam and Eve] ate, so that their shame became apparent unto them and they began to cover themselves with some of the leaves of the Garden. And Adam disobeyed his lord, [and thus] he went astray.[12]

This same narrative recurs in another chapter in the Koran, with added details on the fate of Adam, Eve and Satan: "But Satan misled them, expelled them from the place in which they were; and we said, 'Fall down each one of you a foe unto the other! There shall be for you on earth a habitation and provision for a time.'"[13]

After his sin, Adam is quoted in the Koran as having asked Allah for pardon and forgiveness, and Allah indeed forgave him. "Adam received from his lord words and he [Allah] accepted his repentance. Lo! He is the acceptor of repentance, the merciful.[14] Our first parents as created by Allah [and this applies to all of us] were innocent in matters material as well as spiritual. They knew evil."[15]

In sharing our Christian faith, it is crucial to point out the consequences of the fall that we read in the above two quotations. Some of those consequences are:

First: Adam and Eve became aware of their sexual organs, referred to in the Koran as "their shame." Ask the Muslim why they did not consider their sexual organs shameful before they sinned. In other words, if Adam and Eve were restored to their original innocence and state of grace in the Garden, why do we still consider the exposure of our sexual organs shameful today and cover them with clothing?

Second: Adam and Eve were expelled from the Garden in Paradise. Ask the Muslim, "If Allah forgave them as the Koran states, and the sin was gone, why were they ejected, and all of humanity as result, from Paradise where they dwelt before the fall?" They were expelled, causing all of their descendants to live apart from God, and thus suffer the consequences of Adam and Eve's sin. This is what we call original sin, a condition inherited from Adam and Eve; a position of being separated from God and out of the state of His grace in which He originally intended us to live.

Third: Adam and Eve, now expelled, no longer enjoy the conversations and communion they once had with God. This was a direct result of lack of faith in God's Command.

Fourth: Sin entered the world through Adam's fall. Prior to their sins, they were innocent, since it cannot be said that God created them guilty. This sin was expressed in the next generation when Cain killed Abel. The Koran blames Cain for all of the murders in the world but does not call this original sin. The Muslim never acknowledges that this is the pattern Christians use to identify original sin.

In the Bible, prior to sin, Adam and Eve had opportunity to *confirm* their right standing with God through faith and obedience to His command. They could have affirmed that they were holy, set apart for God, through faith in His Word and their obedience. However, once they disobeyed (sinned), they could not undo the effects of that knowledge; nor could they rid themselves of their *attraction* to sin. They were now pulled *towards* sin. We find this same nature in every human being today. Muslims should recognize these points as indications of original sin in every human being alive.

Muslims justify the sin of Adam based on the Koran's claim that he "forgot to obey" Allah. So Allah forgave Adam. They claim that forgetfulness is the crucial factor in our own struggle against sin, and the main reason why Adam and we sin! I pose a rhetorical question here: What would a court judge say to the criminal who excuses himself, saying he simply forgot the law? Would the judge simply let him go? Obviously the answer is no. Doesn't God's justice require recompense even more so?

Furthermore, the Koran suggests that Adam was *created* with certain degrees of *disposition to sin*. "And we had a Covenant with Adam before, but he forgot and we found in him no resolve."[16] The Koran boldly states that Allah gave *some* free will to humans. "Man, according to the plan of Allah, but in order to fulfill his high destiny, was given free will to limited extent."[17] Here, the reason given for Adam's sin is his "limited free will." The Koran indicates yet another reason: "Indeed, man was created very impatient."[18] Christians cannot imagine blaming God for creating Adam and Eve deficient in any way.

Muhammad's Traditions are another source for Islamic theology. The word for traditions in Arabic is Ahadith, which is plural for Hadith. Ahadith are small little tales or stories representing Muhammad's words and deeds. This is also known as Sunnah. Muhammad states in the Traditions that it is because of Adam we are expelled from Paradise. "You are Adam whose mistake expelled you from Paradise."[19] In contrast, the Koran states that "Every soul draws the [guilt] of its acts on none but itself: no bearer of burdens can bear the burden of another."[20]

Muhammad places the responsibility on Adam for mankind's expulsion from Paradise. Muhammad says that Moses blamed Adam at the gates of heaven when Moses said, "You are the one who made people miserable and turned them out of Paradise."[21] Adam himself confesses one or more times that it was his sin that expelled all humanity from Paradise as he is called upon by the faithful [Muslims] standing at the gates of heaven, crying out, "Our father [Adam], open the gates for us." Adam responds, "And what dismissed you out of Paradise except my sin?"[22]

If the sin of Adam is not inherited by all humanity, how then does Muhammad blame all our sins on Adam's son, Cain? Muhammad says that Cain is indirectly responsible for all the crimes including murders and bloodshed, since he committed the first murder on earth. "Whenever a person is murdered unjustly, there is a share of the burden of that crime on the first son of Adam, for he [Cain] was the first to start the tradition of murdering."[23]

Abdullah Yusuf Ali, in *The Meaning of the Holy Koran*, states that while Adam is a prototype of mankind, his sin "applied to Adam, [and] Eve."[24] Muhammad confirms original sin by implication in the Koran and the Hadith, as does Abdullah Yusuf Ali. *But mainstream Muslims deny this all the way.*

The reason they deny original sin is because they would have to acknowledge our need for a Savior. And Jesus Christ is the only Savior on the horizon.

The question to ask your Muslim neighbor is this: "How are your good deeds sufficient to grant you entry into Heaven, since Adam's good deeds were not enough to keep him there? His one sin drove him [and all of us] out of Paradise."

Our sin is sin against Infinite God, and thus it has infinite implications. Sinful man is both limited and finite, unqualified to repay sin against Infinite God? All of our good deeds are thus insufficient to gain us entry into Paradise.

The objective moral order and balance that were inverted by Adam's sin caused an *infinite gap* between us and God. Such an infinite gap can be closed only by an infinite being. Hence, unless God Himself restored the objective moral order that humans upset, there would be no way for the relationship between God and man to be restored. God Himself provided the path of reconciliation through the shed blood of His Son, Jesus Christ.

CREATED IN THE IMAGE OF GOD

We provided proof that the concept of original sin, and its consequences, is present in Islam. A Muslim believes that he can remove his own sin by asking Allah to forgive him, and/or by doing good deeds.

Scholars have seen many of the verses we will cite from the Koran, yet they have seen no need to join the dots. It has always been considered impossible to "understand" Allah. Instead, they have stressed "submission" to Allah, even if that means suspending your reason and your questions. Some Muslims stress the transcendence of Allah when they want you to quit trying to understand him. They say that finite man cannot understand Divinity. To them, it is blasphemy to think you can understand Allah's nature; these are the ones who stress unquestioning obedience to Allah. Too much questioning of Islam can lead to doubt!

It is OUR duty and responsibility, as ambassadors of Jesus Christ and of the truth of the Eternal God to Muslims, to connect those dots and bring them to a saving knowledge of Jesus Christ. The Muslims are also created in God's Image; and for their sake as well, Jesus Christ went to the cross. Let us imitate His sacred love for the Muslims, one Muslim at a time.

What is the significance of God creating us in His Image, and why it so important for us to know this? As with other theological concepts in Islam, we find both sides of the issue "revealed."

Abu Hamid AL-Ghazali, in his book, *Ihya Ulum Al-Din* (which means the revival of religious science), quotes a Hadith of Muhammad. This comes directly from the book of Genesis: "Allah created Adam in His Image." He describes his 5th reason why man should love Allah: because there is a resemblance between the two.

The notion of the "Image of Allah in Adam" CAN be found in the Koran, in the word "Surat," which can mean "picture" or "Image."

"And We have created you and formed you." The Arabic is Sawarnakoom, which means "shaped you" or "shaped you in the Image." Sorah is the Arabic for picture, or Image. (Koran 7:11. See also 20:102.)

The famous Muslim historian Al-Tabari agrees that man was created in the Image of God. He cites Muhammad's own words that "God created Adam in His Image."[25] Furthermore, Sayyid Hossien Nasr, a respected Islamic scholar originally from Iran, says that "God created man in His Form." Here, form does not mean physical Image, but a reflection of God's Name and Qualities."[26]

It is of extreme importance that we clarify what Christians mean by "created in God's Image." We do not attribute to God any human characteristics. However, God designed us in such a way that we had communion with Him. We are the only creatures that have a moral conscience. We have free will, and the freedom to acknowledge God's laws and His ways. God created us to embody and reflect the dignity and love of God. He gave to us the ability to know Him in intimate ways. We were created to reflect the beauty and truth and goodness of God, the Father. We are not at all a *SOURCE* of this Image. It is the pattern and purpose for which God created us.

PEACEFUL ISLAM

The readers will easily decipher that I intend to go into detail in this chapter, for good reason.

I know that if we want to communicate the Gospel in a way that Muslims can understand, we need to be able to predict how Muslims outside the Islamic world operate and think. It is important to know how they justify their plans to Islamicize the non-Muslim[27] world. We should imitate Muhammad's approach to the unbelievers in like circumstances, since every Muslim considers Muhammad's life to be the pinnacle of evangelism. We Christians imitate, hopefully, the example of Jesus, the Son of the living God. Likewise, Muslims have been taught to look up to Muhammad.

Islamic organizations in non-Muslim countries have as a top priority the evangelization, by hook or by crook, of all non-Muslims. We saw in the 1990's, in exchange for lower oil prices, Clinton agreed to allow Saudi Arabia to open Mosques in virtually every neighborhood. Every major university in the US now has its own Islamic Studies Department, with its dean a Muslim. They learned well from the African-American Studies Departments that they could bring in their "specialists" as professors and organize Muslim students on campus virtually under the radar.

In the West, Muslims are still a minority. Since September 11, 2001, Westerners, in general, are unfamiliar with Islam. Muslim organizations realize this ignorance, and they intend to work around and exploit this ignorance. They have become experts at working the media and using the slogans and rights to their evangelistic ends. Some online Muslim websites claim more than 35,000 converted to Islam in the US in the three years following September 11, 2001.

All Islamic organizations in the West have a hidden agenda, and they ALL share the same dream: to Islamicize the Western societies in every aspect of life. Each organization has its strategy and tactics, which they extract from the example of Muhammad's life. "Islam is a continuous striving to establish the word of Allah on earth, to establish the proper system which brings contentment and bliss to mankind."[28]

The revelation of the Koran to Muhammad began approximately in 610 a.d. in Mecca and continued throughout his life until his death in 632 a.d. During the first three years, Muhammad did not proclaim Islam publicly. These first three years are called the hidden period, where he and his small group of followers gathered together in the house of Al-Arqam Bin Al-Arqam. During the hidden period, Muhammad is said to have confided the revelation to his wife, friends and some close relatives. He, himself, was unsure if he were hearing a revelation from a good angel or a bad angel. His wife, Khadeja, and his uncle, who was a Nestorian Monk, convinced him that he was indeed hearing from a good angel.

In these first few years, he attracted some converts who were considerable figures in Mecca. "His early followers included some close relatives, such as his cousin, Ali ibn Abi Taleb (Caliph 600–61), as well as a few prominent persons in Mecca from influential clans, such as Uthman ibn Affan (Caliph 575–656) of the Umayya clan."[29]

His cousin, Ali, was then a young man who later on became the fourth Caliph (i.e., successor to Muhammad) and the most revered figure, after Muhammad, for Shiites. The socially prominent Uthman was a very rich merchant who purchased many slaves who had been tortured. Uthman is also the father of two of Muhammad's wives; he eventually became the third Caliph, or successor to Muhammad. Abu Bakr, the father of Muhammad's 9-year-old wife, became the first Caliph.

Among those who joined with Muhammad was his uncle Hamza Ibn-Abd Al-Mutalib.

> Hamza, upon hearing that his nephew, Muhammad, was insulted by Abu-Jahel, was furious, searching for Abu-Jahel and finding him among many people, he did not greet anyone standing near Abu-Jahel. He drew his bow and hit Abu-Jahel's face injuring him, and saying, "You insulted my nephew for

being a Muslim. I am one [Muslim] from now, return my insult if you can."[30]

The Islamic lunar calendar begins with the migration of Muhammad from Mecca to Medina.

If the Koran was revealed in 610 a.d., it should be considered the most important date in Islam. Yet it is not. The Islamic calendar does not date from that time, but from the time Muhammad migrated to Medina. This makes us wonder which one is more important in Islam: Is it the Koran or Muhammad?

In the early period, until his migration from Mecca, at 622 a.d., Muhammad did not choose, wisely so, to combat his opponents. He had abundant opponents, whether it was those who disagreed with him in doctrine, as did the Jews and Christians, or whether it was the others who rejected Muhammad's message claiming he was a liar, lunatic, magician, soothsayer, poet, etc.

His evangelistic approach to Jews and Christians in the early period in Mecca was peaceful with conciliatory tones; Muhammad hoped to be recognized by them as the Final Prophet. In his attempt to convert them to Islam, he claimed to worship the same God as the Jews and the Christians. He had his followers bow towards Jerusalem when they prayed. He hoped, minimally, to neutralize the influence of the prominent Jews, since they were men of social and religious prestige in Arabia.

The Christians and Jews were too numerous in Mecca for Muhammad to engage in combat, and wisely so, he avoided open clashes with them. Muhammad's early proclamations of Islam were met with hostility and suspicion by most of the people in Mecca. The Muslims living presently in Western countries take comfort and gain courage, believing that their lives imitate the Prophet's life. The suspicions, and perceived hostility they may encounter only remind them of Muhammad's early life in Mecca.

The Western world is considered to be the very same system of Jahiliyya (ignorance) as Muhammad faced in the early period in Mecca. Some major Islamic figures today state, "Understandably, Muslims in North America are asking questions about strategies for improving the society and bringing about order and sanity to replace the chaos that surrounds them."[31] Muhammad's method of containment of the evils in society around him was patience, perseverance and cunning determination, slowly winning followers, and establishing communications with various tribes in and outside of Mecca.

Muhammad's early followers included slaves, lower-class people, and the oppressed. The slaves initially had been bought by the first Caliph and were offered their freedom if they converted. Once they were "freed," they remained living with other Muslims, and they were encouraged, in return, to wage Jihads and enslave others who would not convert to Islam. At one point, later on, half of the slaves in Mecca converted to Islam to win their freedom and were subsequently recruited to fight the wars on behalf of Muhammad.

Among all of his followers, only the slaves played a major role in dividing Mecca into two factions, since the slave trade was very lucrative. If your master were a non-Muslim, you were free to convert to Islam and run away to "freedom," since *every slave who entered into Islam was free man or woman* equal in rights to all other Muslims. Slavery today is illegal in the non-Muslim world, for the most part.

However, many parts of the Muslim world today still practice slavery. If a slave runs away from a Muslim master, it is considered a *crime possibly punishable by death*. Even if he is a Muslim slave being held by a Muslim master, his prayers will not be heard by Allah unless, and until, he returns to his captivity. Obviously, there is a double standard here.

This double standard was the cunning tactic by which Muhammad won easily the hearts of all the slaves, although he had not yet won all of their conversions. Today, the wedge of racism, and the political and economic disadvantage of African-Americans in prisons is being used to win their conversions to Islam.

The claim of Muhammad that Allah created the white people to go to Heaven and the black people to go to hell, would lead to cries of racism, if the media published it.

> When Allah created Adam, he hit Adam on his right shoulder and the white race came about. And while hitting him on the left shoulder, the black race came about. To those on right, Allah said, to Heaven you go as your dwelling place and to those on the left, he said, to hell you go as your dwelling place.[32]

OUT OF ISLAM, FREE AT LAST

We suggest to all black Muslims that they question their faith, and their Imams, with this statement.

Muhammad had mainly two factions causing him concern. The first group was comprised of pagan Arabs; the second group was the "people of the book," comprised of Jews, Christians and Sabeans. Muhammad developed different strategies for the two groups.

Muhammad often was distressed and hopeless, since his own people, the Arabs, deserted and abandoned him and did not believe he was a messenger of God. Alone and desperate, Muhammad cried and prayed for God's help, asking God to make the way for his people to believe in him. Then came what are known as "the Satanic verses," where Muhammad praised the gods of the pagan Arabs to win their support. In the beginning of Muhammad's path, he exhorted the pagans to worship their three gods, but this got him nowhere.

Muslims believe that the names of three false gods were placed on Muhammad's tongue, and that he was inspired (by Satan) to claim that al-Lat, al-Uzza, and Manat, the third were exalted Gharaniq, whose intercession is approved. It is said that Satan did this to discredit Muhammad.

Lat, Manat and Uzza were three main gods of the Arabs, and their statues presumably were displayed in the Ka'ba. The text where Muhammad praises the false gods cannot be found in the Koran, and yet it is documented by Muhammad's earliest biographers within the first two centuries after his migration to Medina in 622 a.d. Ibn Ishaq, who died in Baghdad c.767 a.d., and Ibn-Hisham, who died c.833 a.d. in Egypt, document Muhammad's acknowledgement of the false gods of the pagan Arabs. It remains a question whether these statements were removed (by someone) from the earliest Koran, since the earliest biographers were seeking to explain why they were there. There is evidence some verses were removed throughout history; we can see written in the Al-Aksa Mosque in Jerusalem a quote from the Koran which cannot be found on its pages today.

The enemies of Muhammad in Mecca were not happy with his concessions, in sanctioning these other pagan gods. He was willing to compromise his claim the Koran was a divine revelation, in return for winning over his pagan opponents in Mecca. To ameliorate the situation, Muhammad stated in the Koran that all previous prophets in history had been tempted by Satan. Since advocacy of other gods is such a big sin in Islam, how is it that their prophet is the *only one* who did this? No other prophet, though all were tempted by Satan, ever acknowledged other gods.

Koran 22:52 "Whenever any messenger or prophet whom we sent before you desired something, Satan interfered with his desire. But Allah abrogates what Satan put there. Then Allah establishes his verses, since he is knowing and wise."

It has been said that Muhammad, upon realizing what he had done, was saddened and full of fear, and yet Allah was ready to abrogate what Satan did through adding another text in Koran 53:21–23: "Al-Lât, al-'Uzzâ and the third, Manât, said, 'Should you have male children and he females, that would be an unfair division. They are only names which you and your ancestors have given them.'"

May we ask here, if the advocacy of worship of any other than Allah is an *unforgivable sin* in Islam, how is it Muhammad was forgiven for doing this? And though Satan at times tempted Jesus and other prophets, the temptation *never* resulted in their advocacy of other gods. The Koran is said to be the perfect revelation of God, so how and why would the perfect word of God (the Koran) come through a sinner Muhammad, but could not be perfectly delivered and preserved for all mankind through Jesus?

How it is possible that a fallen angel, Satan, can overcome Gabriel's word-for-word dictation of the Koran? *This would be proof that an evil angel has the ability to subvert a good angel.* And thus, evil would prevent good, rendering it impotent. If the Koran were the TRUE word of Allah, how is it possible that Satan prevents it from going forth? God's Word is above all and created everything, and a created being cannot prevent it from going forth. *If so, God would be less powerful than His creatures.* It is also said that Satan has no authority over Allah's servant (Koran 16:99–100, 17:65, and 34:2).

Muhammad's early evangelistic tone in the Koran was one of reconciliation, as we stated above. He did not intend to bring about a new religion, but rather to revive what he saw as the faith of Abraham. His initial approach to the Jews and Christians was kind and gentle as we read in the Koran. In fact, it is difficult to distinguish between Muhammad's statements and what was the revelation apart from him, since they seem to be inextricably entwined. Sometimes Muhammad himself appears to be the speaker.

Muhammad claimed that the Allah he worshipped was one and the same as the God of the Jews and Christians. Koran 21:108 reads, "Say: It is only inspired in me *that your Allah is One Allah. Will ye then surrender [unto him]?*" This verse was revealed, according to Muslim scholars and commentators on the Koran, as the well known Abu Al' Al-Mawdawe (1903–1979)[33] in the third stage of Muhammad's early life in Mecca; that is to say, in or around 619–622 a.d.

Muhammad also stated that all Muslims ought to follow his example and believe in the revelations sent to the Jews and Christians. This is to say, Muhammad claimed to believe in the Torah, the Psalms, and the Bible (Injil, in Arabic) as quoted below. He even admonished his followers to seek clarification from the People of the Book (Jews and Christians) whenever the Muslims had questions about the faith. As a matter of fact, even when Muhammad doubted the revelation of the Koran, he was admonished to seek counsel of the Jews and Christians. "If you are in doubt of what we have revealed unto you, then ask the people of the book."[34] Yet Muslims never practice this. The last place they believe they will hear the truth about God is from a Jew or a Christian—unfortunately, for them.

Muhammad tried to say that he and the Jews and Christians worship one and the same God. Koran 21:108 and 29:46 reads, "We believe in that which has been revealed to us and revealed to you, and our Allah and your Allah is one, and to him do we submit."[35] He tried to convince the Jews that he was their final prophet. But the Jews rejected him as a prophet, knowing that all of their prophets have come through the House of Israel.

Muslims today claim Jews, Christians, and Muslims all worship the God of Abraham. However, a quick review of the Koran shows us that the Allah revealed in its pages bears little resemblance to the God of Israel. The Muslims do NOT believe we all worship the same God, but they say so for politically correct and evangelistic reasons. We investigate this matter in a later chapter.

The environment into which Muhammad was born is called Jaheliyya, which means "ignorance." It refers to the darkness and ignorance in which the pre-Islamic Arabs lived, worshipping pagan idols. The concept of Jaheliyya is important for Christians to recognize, since Muslims use the same term in referring to the Western world. It connotes a state of ignorance from which people should be evangelized. Today's radical Muslims, who, in my judgment, are the authentic, idealistic, Muhammad-following Muslims, repeat the concept against the West, whipping crowds into frenzy in the Mosques and on the streets. These radicals mirror Muhammad's hateful tactics as he waged Jihad on his enemies.

Many of the "moderate" Muslims today identify with Muhammad's early life. They exaggerate minute and strained similarities between Islam and Judaism and Christianity, hoping to win over converts. "Moderate" Islamic organizations engage in joint ventures with Jews or Christians, such as inter-religious dialogues, community services, "peace" movements, and legislative efforts aimed at "tolerance." Sometimes they exchange visits and make declarations and public appearances with religious figures among Jews and Christians. The radical Muslims focus their evangelism through violent Jihad, and every Muslim is to follow Muhammad's example in evangelizing the non-believers. Unfortunately, Muhammad provided an example to radicals as well as to moderates.

RADICAL ISLAM

Muhammad's life, theology and attitude all changed like a Jekyll and Hyde when he left Mecca for Medina. Since all the prophets before Muhammad were stoned or killed by Jews—or so he said—why did he lack the faith and perseverance to endure the same at their hands? I note that Muhammad fled Mecca; he literally ran out of town in fear of his life. For Muslims to use the word "migration" in English is only one of their purposeful and skillful uses of the language. Migration connotes a choice, a peaceful, deliberate move from one place to another for the benefits thereof. Muhammad had offended their gods and had divided people in Mecca-he was a source of strife, and everyone wanted him gone. Migration does not clearly cover this aspect of his departure.

The second stage of Muhammad's life started during 622 a.d., when he "migrated" to Medina, which was called Yathrib, and which is called in our modern times as Al-Madina Al-Monawara, or the illuminated city. In this second stage, after Muhammad gave up on converting the masses by the free exchange of ideas, violent Jihad became the call to all Muslims, according to the Koran. Keep in mind, the Koran is the eternal, unchanging word of Allah, and thus, in every age, for all eternity, if the non-believer will *not* convert, he is to be killed.

The much-touted "doctrinal agreement with the Jews and Christians" morphed into extreme doctrinal differences when Muhammad came out of the war of Uhud[36] that the Muslims lost to the people of Mecca. Immediately upon losing this war, Allah revealed to Muhammad that the God of the Jews and Christians *IS NOT* the same as Allah! Now the theological bases were set in place for all non-believers to be de-humanized and conquered through violent Jihads.

Did Allah change His mind? NO, but perhaps Muhammad did. The Eternal God does not change His mind, since He is immutable. Muhammad must have had a change of heart and mind as he was defeated, disgraced, and badly wounded in his war with Mecca. He had lost many brave men, some of who were his relatives, as was Hamza.

Muhammad's shift in attitude and discourse is simply brushed aside by Muslims by stating that "Allah abrogates [nullifies, or changes] whatever He pleases." This is true for human but not true for God because he is immutable.

Even if we agree that God can change His mind, this does not explain Muhammad's shift in attitude from reconciliation to violence and beheading of his enemies. The texts that were revealed in Mecca were never abrogated, as we read in Koran 3:151. "Soon shall we cast terror into the hearts of the unbelievers, for that they joined companions [said Jesus was Divine] with Allah, for which he had sent no authority: their abode will be the fire: And evil is the home of the wrong-doers!" Here, Muhammad places Christians directly in the Muslims' lines of sight for terror.

This shift of attitude is based on Muhammad's relations with the "people of the book," but such shift did not include the pagan Arabs themselves. Muhammad was more than ready to acknowledge their gods; he promoted them.

It is true that Muhammad was persecuted in Mecca, and Muslims claim these persecutions reached a level of threats on his life. But it is also true to Arab nature that he did not like being humiliated. Is it possible that Muhammad's own personality problems caused him to run away and to shift to violence? There was no other prophet before him with such a pattern.

Though many of his followers came from the slave class or were poor, uneducated Arabs, Muhammad took pride in the fact that his uncle, Abu Talib, and many other strong figures had become Muslims. Followers like Hamza, Ali Ibn Abu Talib, Abu Bakr, Uthman Bin Afan, Omer Ibn-Katab, who were all public figures and highly respected, heartened him. Muhammad was also encouraged by support from both of his clans, the Hashim and the Al-Mutallib. The support of his blood relatives, even if they did not agree with every thing Muhammad did, provided him with the loyalty and honor of the clans, which took precedence over all their theological differences.

During his stay in Mecca, Muhammad masterfully turned the lives of the rich people to misery. He offended everyone in his bitter rages. He managed to undermine their sacred practices by pointing out their hypocrisies. He preached about the plight of their slaves, fully angering the rich in Mecca, the virtual Grand Central station for the slave trade.

Muhammad remained married to his first wife, Khadeja, until her death. After her death, he began to take on multiple wives. Upon the death of two of the most important people in his life, his wife, Khadeja, and his uncle, Abu-Talib, in or around 619 a.d., he was finished in Mecca. His uncle had been his main source of emotional support and his main protector. Abu-Talib, although never having embraced the prophet's message, had nonetheless used the solidarity of the Hashim clan to defend Muhammad.

When Muhammad's attempt to win the conversions of his clan did not work, he was openly mocked. The public's suspicion of his message's Divine authenticity hardened. Muhammad answered by a scathing attack on the gods of Mecca. First, he had told them their gods were ok; now he was fiercely opposing those gods as idols. The Arabs of Mecca chose to approach Muhammad's uncle, Abu-Talib, in an effort to calm down his nephew. After all, he was insulting their gods, disturbing their way of life, and generally freaking out the established gentry by his outrageous claims.

In one more attempt to turn Muhammad from his mission to destroy their way of life, they implored his respected uncle to convince Muhammad to stop ridiculing their gods and all that was sacred to them. In return, the people of Mecca offered to make him the richest in town, and if Muhammad agreed to calm down, they offered to install him as their chief.

Muhammad's response was, "If they give me the sun on my right hand and the moon on the other hand, just to leave what I am doing, I will not." Muhammad's resistance gave the gentry of Mecca no obvious alternative but to eliminate him. But how could they kill Muhammad and risk a war with Muhammad's clan? Not a single tribe by itself could afford such a war. They had already attempted unsuccessfully to cut all ties of marriage and trade with Muhammad's clan, to no avail.

What the leaders decided upon was a brilliant plan to kill Muhammad. They chose one young strong man from each of their allied clans to attack Muhammad in his bed while he slept. With one strike, in which all these young warriors would participate, they could scatter the responsibility for the blood of Muhammad among more clans than his tribe could handle.

According to the Muslim historian Al-Tabare, "The angel Gabriel came to Muhammad and told him, 'do not stay this evening in your bed.'"[37] Muhammad took off from the town with his closest friend, Abu-Bakr, and this is purported to be the reason for his "migration" to Yathrib [Medina] in 622 a.d. in the third month of the lunar calendar. He had already sent his followers ahead to Medina and commanded his followers who fled to Ethiopia to return to Medina, for Allah provided for them in Medina a shelter. His wife, Khadeja, had secured a refuge for him in Medina shortly before her death.

Islamic scholars assert that when Muhammad arrived in Medina, the city was torn apart by quarrels and skirmishes between two of the major Bedouin tribes, the Aws and the Khazraj. Though this may have been the case, we can surmise that Muhammad offered to bring them together. However, knowing Muhammad's cunning, he most likely used their differences to his advantage where possible, as well. Both classic and contemporary Muslim historians say that he brought peace, but we have only their side of the story. "It was only about the time when the prophet announced his mission at Mecca that these tribes, after long years of continuous warfare, entered on a period of comparative peace."[38] He announced that he was leaving to go to Medina, using the pretext that he was asked to come to Medina as a mediator. He announced this to the people in Mecca so that it would not appear that he was fleeing Mecca, but we note that he departed Mecca under cover of darkness.

Quarrels existed in Medina not only before the arrival of Muhammad, but new quarrels took place *because* Muhammad came to town. As Muhammad arrived, Medina was smoldering with rivalries. There were the two quarrelling main Arab tribes, the Muhajirun ("immigrants," i.e., the believers who had immigrated to Medina from Mecca or elsewhere) and the Ansar ("helpers," i.e., Muhammad's first followers in Medina). These squabbling tribes had invited Muhammad, with his followers, to take refuge with them. There was also strife between some of Medina's Jews and the new Muslim believers (sic).[39]

Two tribes are recorded to have asked Muhammad to mediate between them. Yet we have only ten people who were called Ansar. These were those who supported Muhammad and had become Muslims while on their annual pilgrimage to Mecca. Is it possible that these two "tribes" were a majority of the people in Medina? Most likely the two tribes were smaller ones, but some claim today that a majority of inhabitants of Medina were already Muslim when Muhammad arrived. It is doubtful.

These questions may seem obscure and irrelevant to the Christian who wants to share his faith with a Muslim. However, it is important to understand that Muhammad changed not only his theology and tactics, but he shifted his location to suit his agenda. Readers will see clearly the shift of his theology when I deal with the chapters on the Holy Spirit and God.

Muhammad, when he was in Mecca, reached out with a tone of reconciliation and peace. He even addressed the Christians as having the same God as he did. Once he had the upper hand, however, along with some manpower in Medina, everything changed. He became violent. He demanded submission; he waged wars (Jihads) and exhibited a completely different nature than what he had in Mecca. This is very important for Muslims to know, and for Christians to highly emphasize.

Christendom offered a choice between conversion, or exile, apostasy and death to Jews and Muslims in Catholic Spain. Some quasi-intellectuals wrongly state that Jews under Islam fared better through the centuries than they have in recent modern Europe, saying that they were not generally called to martyrdom for their faith.

However, this view is intellectually dishonest at best. The view that Jews fared better under Islam than under Christendom proves the adherent either ignorant of, or unwilling to concede the bloody history of Islam. The purpose of this book is not to explore in great depth this bloody history, but it is rather to expose the theological tenets that permanently sanction the use of fear as a weapon to spread Islam. The unique contribution of Muhammad to the history of forced conversions is that he gave his new religion Divine dimensions of violence and repression, claiming that Allah himself wills the Jihad. The world today sees the violent results of such a belief.

The Muslims bring up the Crusades whenever the subject of Jihad is raised. The Crusades were *a reaction* to the Muslims' actions in overrunning the Holy Land. As I stated earlier, we should not confuse the theology with the practice. As we look at Islam, we see in its very theology a prescription for violence and killing. Their holy books claim it is the word of Allah that all Jews and Christians convert, or be killed. The religion ascribes to Allah the desire to kill off every non-believer makes Islam unique among religions.

The angel Gabriel is said to have recited to Muhammad, "When you are in doubt in what we have revealed unto you, then ask the people of the book." Muhammad failed to do so.

Convenient to Muhammad's growing ambitions, Gabriel is further said to recite, "Kill the non-believers." Amazingly, to my mind, the angel was there just in the knick of time, ready to justify Muhammad's shift of attitude and doctrines!

As I continued to study Islam in my years in Iraq, I read more of Muhammad's blatant insults, fanatical patterns and expedient tactics. I was astonished to see that the angel Gabriel was right behind, revealing new proclamations on what Muhammad did the day before. This same Gabriel had not been in any rush to justify other prophets before. Rather, the Jewish prophets suffered for delivering prophecy and in many cases were condemned for speaking God's Word. I continued to give Islam the benefit of the doubt, thinking that I may have read the wrong scholar. To my dismay, I found that all the scholars thought alike, and the pages of the Koran attested to my conclusions. All of this caused me serious doubt about the claim the Koran was the word of Allah.

I began to ponder why others in history referred to Islam as "Muhammadanism." It was becoming more obvious that Islam was more a cult of Muhammad than anything else. It prompted me to look into the Jewish and Christian faiths as a result. Of course this was highly discouraged, and officially curtailed. The librarians knew me well because I was constantly there. I befriended them, and although they were required to write down what someone was borrowing, they overlooked their responsibilities. Among the Kurds, this is normal... we could read whatever we wanted. But in the rest of Iraq—the Iraq that I grew up in—people loved to break the rules and not abide by the edicts of the central government of Saddam.

To prove the claim that the Koran is the word-for-word dictation of Allah, the Koran should be consistent and of the same theology throughout, no matter the location of the prophet. The reality of Muhammad's life is anything but consistent, and his theology and morals changed drastically from place to place. Muhammad's life itself brings into question for the intellectual Muslim, whether the Koran is of Divine origin or not. Indeed, many Muslims doubt it and even say so, but they are prohibited from finding another faith.

To return to our subject, the truth is that not every one in Medina was comfortable with Muhammad's presence or his new theology, which he claimed was the faith of Abraham. Abraham is said to be the first Muslim[40] ... Well, where does this leave Noah, Elijah, and Adam?

By now, Muhammad's presence in Medina had begun to instill fear in the community. Muhammad's own admission and various texts in the Koran convey the idea. There were those in Medina called Munafeqeen (hypocrites) by Muhammad; these converted to Islam out of fear rather than faith. Muslim scholars insist that the converts in Medina were in the minority.[41] If they were a minority, their conversions would have gone relatively unnoticed. But the Muslims insist that these conversions were publicly well known. Perhaps the Muslims who claim the converts were in the minority are counting only the ones who were "true" converts to the faith; masses of others must have converted publicly out of fear, I would assert.

Muhammad proceeded with a tactic to divide and conquer in Medina. Certainly the attraction of a superior status as Arabs, coupled with the "Divine" mandate to steal, kill and destroy the non-Muslim made many Arabs convert for self-serving motives. No one had to turn the other cheek or love one's enemies. No one was called to sacrifice oneself for others. Quite the reverse was now available, and it was a new and final religion! You could do away with your enemies and not go to confession afterward! In fact, you would gain "entry to Paradise" by killing the non-Muslim.

The first two years that Muhammad was in Medina, he still prayed towards Jerusalem. But once he took on the Jews and raided their caravans in Jihad, he switched the direction of prayer towards Mecca. This was a radical shift, because no longer was the Allah of Muhammad the same as the God of Israel. Muhammad claimed that Abraham and Ishmael had built Mecca. He added this prestige for Mecca, praying towards it as the holiest of cities! The Bedouins saw now, that they would be written forever into the Divine code of Islam. It would give Bedouin Mecca, rather than Jerusalem, a dignity above all others. Everything was in place to persuade the Arabs.

The Ansar (partisans) were familiar with the concept of one God, since they lived amongst the Jews in Medina, who composed the majority of the city. The Christian populations living there also believed in one God. The Ansar supporters eventually brought 75 men to follow Muhammad, and they entered into a treaty with the prophet called Baye'aht Al-Aqaba. These 75 men came from the same locale as the relatives of Muhammad's wife, Khadeja, lived. Her tribe had converted, so it is fair to assume that they may have been members of Khadeja's clan.

In the treaty of Aqaba, the Ansar (partisans, or supporters) accepted Muhammad as a prophet and took an oath to defend him if he were attacked. They pledged to provide refuge for the other followers, as well as a pledge to allow the Jews to practice their faith freely, though the Jews had not entered into the treaty of Aqaba.

Soon after his arrival in Medina, Muhammad ordered a series of raids (Jihads) on the merchant caravans coming north from Mecca along the busy trade route. Medina was a strategic and economic trade center between Syria and Mecca, and Muhammad used it to his full advantage. The Muhajareen (who had followed Muhammad to Medina) joined in the earliest Jihads of Muhammad. They needed income to gain independence from the Ansar (supporters who were their hosts in Medina,) and to replace whatever they had lost in Mecca before they fled. Muhammad was gradually building his base, primarily through the material gains that were to be had by those who joined him in his Jihads.

Eventually, Mecca itself had to fight Muhammad; his stranglehold was now in place along the trade route that they needed for their livelihood. Muhammad launched raid after raid against their caravans, seizing valuable booty and hostages, disrupting the commercial lifeblood of Mecca.[42] The Muslims fought three major wars against Mecca: at Badr (624 a.d.), and again at Uhud (625 a.d.), and again at Khandaq (627 a.d.).

There were no less than 22 assault raids according to Ibn-Al-Tabari, not counting the Jihads that were carried out by other Muslim commanders during Muhammad's eight years in Medina. These raids were no less than terrorist attacks, and they caused many to be willing to do anything to bring peace with the prophet Muhammad.

Muhammad's approach towards the Jews of Medina was no less a cause of fright than he had been in Mecca. His hostile tactics were well calculated, and what he demanded did not please the Jews at all. Now, in Medina, he was in no mood to be peaceful with the Jews.

The Jews were a major power in Medina, comprising one third to one half of the population. They had two of the most powerful tribes in Medina, Banu-Nadir and Banu-Qunayqa. Unfortunately, both of these Jewish tribes were robbed of their possessions, and the few survivors were expelled from Arabia. They had their property and valuables distributed among the Muslims, including their wives and children, who became slaves to their new Muslim masters.

Some Jewish thinkers today would rather say they had it easier under Islam than under Christendom, but this is only because they are ignorant of a long history of facts.

Muhammad began by lying about the Jews. He envied their goods, coveted their wives, stole their property, bore false witness against them, blasphemed their God, and killed them outright. The Jews could not have accepted Muhammad's claim to be a prophet to the Jews, since he was breaking every one of the Ten Commandments. What other prophet truly sent by God would have chosen to do so? Numerous totalitarian states in history have begun exactly as Muhammad did. Fanatical leaders turned the people's eyes toward anti-Semitism, and their hearts toward extermination of the Jews. Today is no different, as I do not need to remind the reader.

Once he had the upper hand and the manpower, Muhammad became the arch-tyrant. He extorted treaties from various tribes, forcing them to convert to Islam or face death. Finally, he would have his way, and people would have to acknowledge he was the final prophet! No sooner had he achieved a bloody foothold, he turned his ambitions and vision to other lands, and he never looked back on his early peaceful methods. Muhammad decided Islam would be spread through violent Jihads, and he found victory ONLY at the end of a sword.

How can anyone say that he morally surpasses all the other prophets, including the sinless Jesus in the Koran? Since fanatical Muslims believe that Muhammad is the moral apex of all prophets, and they follow his later bloody example, they have no qualms about the *death, torture, and beheading of the infidel.*

Muhammad's disciples did not have to give up their possessions to follow him. Nor did they give up their lives. This is quite opposite from Jesus' exhortation to His followers, to renounce worldly possessions, to sell them and give the money to the poor, to pick up their cross and follow Him. He who will not pick up his cross and follow Him, Jesus said is unworthy to be His disciple. But Muhammad's followers had (and still have) no such calling. They lived as filthy rich masters and overlords. They were free to rob and steal from the non-Muslim in the name of Allah. And thus they did. When we examine and compare the example of Muhammad with that of Jesus, we see opposite ends of the spectrum.

Was this Muhammad, once in Medina, the same man who earlier placed God first in his life? Did Muhammad lose his way from all the humiliation and rejection he elicited in Mecca? What would turn him into such a violent fanatic? We need to examine this, since so many millions follow his example on the earth today. In looking at the theology of Islam, we see that it differs in a crucial way from other religions and does not stand on its merits as the ultimate moral religion. We could say that other world religions seek peace through promoting respect for non-believers. The later stages of Muhammad's life example do not promote respect for non-believers, but rather the elimination of the non-believer.

Muhammad's evangelistic slogans are in use on college campuses, in high schools, and mosques across America today, in an effort to confuse both Western Christians and Jews. Islam is said to be a religion of "peace." They recite, "Our God and your God are one and unto him we surrender." But they *do not* believe that the non-believer and the Muslim worship the same Allah. If we, the non-believers worship the same God, why do Muslims make the effort to convert us?

The Muslims consider it their duty to "migrate" and spread Islam wherever they go. When Muslims are in the minority, they follow one set of rules to change the society around them and to keep from causing alarm about their real agenda. They participate in college religious debates and attempt to win converts in a peaceful way. But once they have immigrated enough to form more than 10% of a non-Muslim nation, their tactics change.

In Europe, for example, the immigrant Muslim community has reached the 10% threshold. We hear of Muslim gangs of young men riding in cars in France, shooting at police stations. In the Netherlands, Muslims have committed crimes against the politicians and prominent persons who dare to speak out against Islam. In England, the call is for the legal system to be changed to Sharia, or Islamic law, and now the Muslims did not hide the fact that they demand England become a Muslim state. Never underestimate what Muslims say is their agenda. They mean it. We have 9/11 in the USA, 7/7 in Britain, and 3/11 in Spain, as reminders.

Violent Jihad becomes the norm for radicals once the Muslim community establishes its numbers. The radicals seek to activate the Muslim population living peacefully in their adopted lands. It is easy to see the examples of this in so many Western nations today. Muhammad is the pattern to be imitated, and thus, they argue, all true Muslims should be following his ways by *furthering the cause of Jihad*.

Mosques and universities in the West are often recruiting grounds for young warriors in the spread of Islam. Even certain businesses operate as a cover to recruit young terrorists. There is pressure exerted on Western Muslim students to "become serious" about the faith. It is noteworthy that Johnnie Walker, the young American found fighting with the Taliban in Afghanistan, was recruited from a California high school.

I knew a Kurdish girl who was studying in a college in Virginia in 1998. Whenever she went to the college library to study, some male Muslim students would approach her and threaten her if she did not start wearing a veil. They asked how she had money to go to school, implying that perhaps she was a prostitute. They asked her all sorts of personal questions about who she lived here with and whether she had brothers, and she began to fear for her life. Muslim radicals exert constant pressure on the Muslim Diaspora to "measure up," or be seen as an unbeliever. These were Muslim males who did not know her personally but felt free to terrorize her in the name of Islam.

Because radicals are determined to set the agenda for all Muslims, moderates in the West are expected to participate in Jihad *materially and otherwise*. Many Muslim businesses have money extorted from them by those who expect them to support the "cause of Islam." One Jihad that women are expected to join is to have many Muslim children. The birth rates in the West have declined among traditional groups, but Muslims who have "migrated" around the world today are not slowing in their birth rates whatsoever.

To return to our examination of Muhammad's life in Medina, we see he made numerous changes to the theology of Islam. For example, now the direction of prayers was to be toward Mecca, facing the city where Muhammad began to preach. He began to adopt and incorporate and alter rituals and traditions within Judaism and Christianity. He worked now to form a unique religion, rather than present himself as a prophet to the established religions. Muslims were required to commemorate the Koran by fasting during Ramadan. He knew that the Jews fasted to commemorate specific miracles of God, as Al-Tabri in his book *The History of the Nations and Kings* attests.

Muhammad copied wholesale from the people of the book. He adopted what he saw as "religious practice" from the Jews, introducing rituals to Islam similar to those he had heard from rabbis. The very concept of praying towards a holy city was taken from the Jews. He instituted precise ritualistic washings before prayer. Muslims could not eat pork, just as the Jews had always treated pork as unclean. And Muhammad adopted many theological concepts from Christianity in order to claim superiority and finality of revelation. He was intent upon forming a completely new religion that would override the previous ones.

With this new religion came entirely new sets of rules, a new world vision, and a new command to wipe out anyone who would not convert.

MUHAMMAD FORMS A NEW RELIGION

The people of the book (Jews and Christians) had not recognized Muhammad as their prophet, so he stole customs and rites from their faiths. He believed he needed to surpass the stature of previous prophets, including Jesus, so he claimed similar miracles happened to him, but without a single eyewitness. Jesus Christ entered Jerusalem on Palm Sunday, riding on a donkey, while the people waved palms as He passed. Muslims claim Muhammad was received in the same way in Medina. Muhammad even went on to claim he, himself, was the Holy Spirit! Had the computers existed at the time of Muhammad, he would have been a master at copy and paste.

His followers claimed that he ascended into Heaven from the top of the Dome of the Rock in Jerusalem, and he spoke to Allah, interceding for the Muslims. No eyewitnesses were presented for this, and no one could establish his absence from Medina. There are legends that he visited Damascus years before, and could have possibly visited Jerusalem in his earlier days. But once he had proclaimed himself a prophet, there is no evidence he ever traveled there. Muhammad is said to have gained for the Muslims (in this ascendancy in Jerusalem) a permanent mercy from Allah. But, this Allah is no longer the same as the one the Jews and Christians worship, the God of Israel.

Muhammad claimed that he received the revelation of the Koran in a cave. Again, there were no eyewitnesses. He was married to Khadeja, and legend has it that he had a custom of visiting the cave areas. He returned one day, shivering, and Khadeja brought him a blanket. He heard a voice, but he had not seen a thing. Muhammad was worried he was becoming insane. Khadeja, according to custom, told him that it was Gabriel, a good angel, who had spoken to him. The Nestorian Monk who earlier had married Khadeja to Muhammad, further convinced Muhammad he had heard from the angel Gabriel, and that Muhammad was indeed a prophet.

Jesus had thousands and thousands of eyewitnesses for His miracles. He fed the five thousand, and He walked on water. He calmed the storms, and He read people's thoughts. Not only were there eyewitnesses among His disciples, but *the unbelieving* Pharisees and Romans also saw what Jesus did. And thousands saw Him die and many hundreds saw Him resurrected!

There were eyewitnesses to the parting of the Red Sea, and there were eyewitnesses to Moses' miracles in Pharaoh's palace. There were eyewitnesses to the Shekinah Glory that radiated on Moses' face when he came down from Mt. Sinai. Many thousands followed the pillar of cloud by day, and the pillar of fire by night in the wilderness while God led His people through the desert.

The inability of Muhammad to produce a single miracle, as a threshold of proof for his claims to be a prophet, leaves us with clear comparisons. Jesus, as the Koran admits, exercised miracle after miracle in His lifetime.

He raised the dead, which ONLY God Himself has the right to govern . . . Obviously, Allah did not bestow upon Muhammad the ability to raise the dead, though God gave this to Elijah. Jesus Christ's miracles[43] were preludes for what is at hand, the Kingdom of God.

There were eyewitnesses to Gideon's miraculous victories on the battlefield. The book of Hebrews, Chapter 11, is a litany of miracles that Christians have experienced. Many more have continued down through the ages, and healings and astounding deeds are done before eyewitnesses (many unbelievers) around the world today because *Jesus Christ is STILL producing them!*

Miracles are not something that God hides from people; *they are given as a testimony to the presence of God.* It is noteworthy that no one ever saw Muhammad produce a single miracle; nor did he ever claim he could perform any miracles. Muslims who followed after Muhammad had to compete with God Himself if they wanted to say the Koran was a Divine miracle. So, legend has it that Muhammad did have miracles.

The Koran claims that there is no compulsion in religion. This means no one should be forced to convert, nor should they be restrained from leaving a religion into which they were born. Since this is in the Koran, why have whole nations been forced into Islam, or massacred? If there is no compulsion, why do they forcefully prohibit conversions to other faiths? Is the conscience of man of no importance to the Muslim religion? If, as the Muslims claim, Muslims have free will, why would they deprive any Muslim from reading the Bible, or from converting to Christianity? Why is this called apostasy, a high crime worthy of death? If Allah gave mankind free will, how is it this free will is suppressed, especially by people claiming to be Muslim themselves? Do these Muslim leaders think they have the right to abrogate Allah's gift? Where the Spirit of God is, there is freedom. Jesus never silenced His opposition. And it is God's Way to force faith.

Christians welcome debate, because we believe the Holy Spirit is capable of speaking to the conscience of man and revealing the truth of God and Jesus Christ to the hearer. But the Muslim is not encouraged to listen to his "conscience" or to question, since that can lead to apostasy, or rejection of Islam. Muslim nations do not permit non-Muslims to evangelize. Even Christians born in Middle Eastern countries are sentenced to death if they speak to a Muslim in such a way as to try to lead him out of Islam.

Every Muslim nation's legal system forbids public questioning of, or criticism of the faith (blasphemy); every critic is silenced or killed.

Furthermore, to those who say Islam is a religion of peace, we ask them to offer one piece of history indicating Islam has been spread successfully through honest and peaceful discussion.[44] The argument may be made that Muslims today in the West *are* converting Western people to Islam, but most of these conversions are NOT done by fully exposing the tenets of Islam to the new convert. Islam is taught in a palatable form, leaving out much of what we cover in this book. Conversions to Islam are won by using Western concepts and imitating Western religious doctrine. Most of the Koran remains unknown by those Muslims born into the faith and remains unknown, especially to new converts.

The hostility in Islam is attractive only to the very few who are prone to violence in the first place and see in Islam a chance to vent their hatred of society in general. These would include those who become terrorists or radical Muslims. Radical Muslims are attracted by the appeal of a male-dominated society and afterlife, to the pride and arrogance of a superior and final prophet, and to the utter absence of self-abandonment or humility.

The followers of Muhammad enriched themselves and lived more luxuriously than all others around them. They invaded lands that previously were Christian or Jewish, Hindi or Buddhist. They invaded Egypt, and the rest of northern Africa, and stole their resources. They invaded Spain and Europe, all the way to Vienna, where the Turks were turned back on the infamous date of September 11, centuries ago. The appeal of material gain (booty) still motivates the bloodthirsty to attack the poor today. Muslims all around the Kurdish nation have stolen, and continue to this day, to steal Kurdish resources, Kurdish oil, and their possessions. Bedouin Arabs and other tribes have stolen lands, oil, and wealth from previous peoples who had lived in the Middle East for centuries. The Arab entitlement mentality is written into Islam.

In the West, Islam works to compete with Christianity by imitating it. Islamic evangelists seem to offer a religion where material things can be shunned in the name of "purity and holiness." They seek to offer everything the new recruit *thought* he had before, but MORE. The new Western converts to radical Islam are persuaded to forsake all (copying what Jesus said) for the sake of Jihad. However, most new converts are attracted by the claims of "peaceful Islam," wherein strict sexual mores and rituals seem to offer brotherhood, racial equality, and "peace." As I stated earlier, Islam seems to provide a holy way of life in its call to prayer five times a day. But *Christians are to pray unceasingly.* Islam, as it stands on the books, does not surpass either Christianity or Judaism in morals, methods, or in spirit. New converts to Islam are *not* coming from the practicing Christians or Jews who know the real God of Israel.

The inability of Muhammad to produce a single miracle, as a threshold of proof for his claims to have been a prophet, left us with clear comparisons. Jesus, as the Koran admits, exercised miracle after miracle in His lifetime. He raised the dead, which, according to Islam, ONLY God Himself has the right to grant . . . Obviously, Allah did not bestow upon Muhammad the ability to raise the dead, though God provided this to Elijah. Jesus Christ's miracles were mere preludes for what is at hand, the Kingdom of God.

Muslims are not stupid. They are simply blinded. They retort that the Koran itself is the miracle of Muhammad. They say it was revealed in pure Arabic language. However, the Koran is filled with non-Arabic words and verbs. Pre-Islamic Arabic poetry is by far more eloquent than the Koran itself. There are tens of synonyms for "sword" and "camel" but not a single word in Arabic for "citizen." The closest equivalent will be "patriot." Even the word "freedom" does not refer to freedom of thought or the freedom of individuals, but it is used exclusively in reference to slaves.

Another response Muslims offer is that the Bible can be doubted, since it was written 30, 60, and 100 years after Jesus' death and resurrection. But they do not remember that Muhammad was illiterate, and his biography itself was compiled in 767 a.d.—100 years after his death. Even the *collection* of the Koran was not finished until 75 years after his death. *They claim that the Arab Bedouins had a very strong memory, more than most.* If this were the case, then wouldn't Allah have endowed Adam with the strongest memory of all so that Adam would not forget the commandment, considering the consequences for all mankind?

When we dialogue with the Muslims, eventually we will encounter their Mediterranean temper and their tendency to violent reaction. They tend to spiritualize every aspect of life, disregarding reason and intellect.

The secular West, in contrast, often intellectualizes to such an extent that the spiritual aspects of faith no longer are valued.

The problems, as I have written them, were paramount for me, as a Muslim. Nowhere could I find an intellectually honest treatise of Islam that resolved its contradictions and shifts in theology. No matter which scholar I read, the scholars simply brushed aside these problems by reiterating Muhammad's Koran and Hadith. *Even birds can be taught to repeat and recite verses.*

There is ONLY ONE WAY for man to be with God eternally, and that is through the shed blood of Jesus Christ. So seize the opportunity while you are here on earth, and you will have life more abundantly here and eternal life with God in Heaven hereafter.

Muslims love to say that the Islamic scholars made crucial contributions to the world. Some did, but the massive work was TRANSLATED from Latin to Arabic by Jewish and Christian scholars The contributions were originally in Latin, much of them made by Christians and Jews, not Muslims themselves. The Arabs try to "name it and claim it," but the truth is, Arabs did not initiate these contributions. Arabs did not "preserve" mathematics or the ancient scholars' works as much as the Catholic Church preserved them through the "Dark Ages."

Individuals in Christianity are called to utilize material but never to be possessed by it. In Islam, material possessions connote the favor of God. In Christianity, the believer is exhorted to PRAY FOR THE ENEMIES, not to behead them on TV and the Internet with a sword. Christianity is not about praying five times a day but about praying UNCEASINGLY, nonstop. Islam tends to be self-centered, self-absorbed and self-contained, while Christianity is about total self-abandonment.

It is the failure of the Christians to recognize these crucial differences and emphasize them.

The majority of Christians appear to be weak when they fail to be bold examples of Christ. The Christian faith is not considered to be true by Muslims if it is not adamantly defended. The faith appears weak when Christians shrink back. It is not tolerance and compromise that leads a Muslim to Christ but PROCLAIMING JESUS AND HIS CRUCIFIXION that will convert the Muslims! The challenge to all Christians today is to *LIVE THE FAITH*, or forever be responsible for not bearing witness to the *POWER of the Gospel to change the world.*

World leaders proclaim that Islam is a religion of peace. But this is for political purposes. It does not make Islam so. The history of Islam proves that it is *ANYTHING* but a religion of peace. Show me one Islamic nation that lived in peace longer than ten years with its Muslims neighbors, and, or, within its own borders. We could spend Eternity looking for the example. *THIS IS NOT THEOLOGY.* It is history.

THE WARS WITH THE JEWS

Relations with the Jews deteriorated once they had rejected Muhammad as their prophet. Muhammad previously acknowledged in Mecca that all prophets come through the Jews.

"We gave him [Abraham] Isaac and Jacob and bestowed on his descendants prophethood"

(Koran 29:27). We note here that Isaac is revealed and not Ishmael.

Muslim scholars hold that this text was abrogated or nullified by Gabriel, and that the replacement for prophets all coming from the Jews can be found in the Koran in

Ankabout [the spider]. This verse refers to the cave where Muhammad hid with his friend shortly before fleeing from Mecca. (See also Koran 45:16.)

Clearly, Muhammad was deeply disappointed in the Jews; he expected them to wholesale convert whether or not their Scriptures pointed to him. He asserted that their Scriptures did indeed verify he was a prophet, but that these verses had somehow been purposely "deleted." Regardless, Muhammad felt, perhaps sincerely, that he said and did nothing contrary to Scripture. He was illiterate, and thus had limited knowledge of Judaism. The Jews often regarded Muhammad as a fanatic and an opportunist.

Muhammad began his attacks on the Jews with lies. He spread rumors that they had changed the words of God and tampered with the Torah and the Psalms.[45] Koran 4:46 reads, "Some of those who are Jews change words from their context." This was revealed to Muhammad right after his initial failure to win over the Jews. Growing increasingly bitter, he threatened and attacked the Jews with lies long before his violent Jihads began. He hoped that causing the Jews mortal fear, they would finally cave in.

Muhammad laid doctrinal grounds (based on false witness) for his attack on the Jews. He demanded that his faithful followers agree to take every word he said as "the word of Allah."

He had now clouded any distinction between the revelation, and his own words. His words, coming from a frail and bitter human being, were now to be seen as Divine revelation. He had always claimed to be a sinner, but now, his word was larger than life. Thus, the days of the Jews in Arabia were fast coming to an end.

Muslim historians and commentators of the Koran see no fault in their treatment of the Jews in Medina or elsewhere in the Middle East. It is also unfair to say that Muhammad and his followers were the only ones who were aggressive; that would be an inaccurate claim. But to fault the victim of aggression, for responding in a forceful way, is wrong. Our own laws acknowledge that killing someone in self-defense is permissible. The Jews have historically been forced into wars, or face extermination. To blame them for self-defense, and call it aggression, is not honest whatsoever.

However, whether or not Jews successfully defended their heritage, they tried to remain faithful to the God of Israel and their sacred Scriptures in the face of a formidable enemy. Muhammad began his ministry with sincere humility, though he was later emotionally crushed by rejection. His Bedouin Arab answer was to become enraged with a false pride and anger that has cost millions of innocent lives through the ages.

Jews and Muslims and Christians alive today have no guilt or responsibility for what previous generations did 1,400 years ago. To believe that we are responsible for any previous generations' suffering, is one error that fuels the fires of hatred today. It is high time for historical grudges to be dropped. People alive today cannot rightfully seek revenge for insults or aggressions that occurred generations, or centuries before. Besides, revenge and aggression are not what God approves for us; He is God, and all vengeance is His.

The last verbal attack was a warning (v. 47) to the Jews given before the Banu Nadir[46] were exiled from Al-Madinah in Rabi'-ul Awwal[47], A.H.[48] From this, it may safely be concluded that the discourse containing v. 47 must have been revealed some time before the 622 date."[49]

Between 624 and 625 a.d., relations between Muhammad and the Jews spiraled downward for a number of reasons. The Jews are said to have enticed and supported others in Mecca to fight Muhammad, and the Jews who made agreements with him are said to have failed to keep their promises. Muhammad, incensed at betrayal, gathered the Banu Qunayqa' in the market square and warned them,

> "O, Jewish people, be careful of Allah's revenge [that] fell upon the Meccans. You know that I am the prophet sent by Allah; you find it in your book and in God's Covenant with you." and they responded, "O, Muhammad, do you think we are as your people? Do not be deceived because you fought with people who had no experience in war, and you took advantage of that . . . if you fight against us, by God, you will know who we are."[50]

Muhammad was quite fearful of the Banu Qunayqa' tribe. Gabriel revealed to him right after his fear became evident that, "If you fear treachery from any group, throw back to them [their Covenant] on equal terms [there will be no Covenant between you and them.] Certainly Allah does not like the treacherous"(Koran 8:58).

Muhammad's gruesome siege on the Banu Qunaqa' clan lasted until they surrendered unconditionally. Muslims and Muhammad stole all of their possessions. Even their Jewish wives and children were taken as slaves. Those who had fought Muhammad were forced to convert or face slaughter. This marked the end of this Jewish clan. Ever since, surrender to Muslims has meant the same devastation . . . slavery, poverty, and eradication.

Poetry was, and still is, used in the Middle East as a tool to enhance, support, and even belittle others. It can build up the morale of the people or rally people behind certain public events or matter(s) of concern. This was true at the time of Muhammad also, and its use was not exclusive to the Arabs alone. Some of the Jewish poets attacked Muhammad through their poetry, and they successfully enticed the people of Mecca to wage war on Muhammad. For this, Muhammad killed three of these poets, between 624 and 625 a.d. The poets were said to be waging war, since their voices were considered to be the jewels and the pride of a tribe.

Muhammad not only lied about the Jews, but he called the Jews apes and pigs and put this into the so-called Divine revelation (Koran 2:65,

5:60, 7:166). The Jews of Nadir and Wa'el (in Medina, according to Muslim commentators) formed an alliance to fight back. They enticed others in Mecca to join with them in their fight against Muhammad. We do not possess any other sources that give an independent account of what occurred.

Koran 4:47, says, "O you who have been given the Scripture! Believe in what we have revealed confirming what is with you before we efface faces and turn them hind wards, or curse them as we cursed the Sabbath breakers." A. A. Al-Mawdawe in commenting on says,

> Bani Nadir, who were showing a hostile and menacing attitude, in spite of the peace treaties they had made with the Muslims, were openly siding with the enemies of Islam and hatching plots against the Holy Prophet and the Muslim Community even at Al-Madinah itself. They were taken to task for their inimical behavior and given a final warning to change their attitude, and were at last exiled from Al-Madinah on account of their misconduct.[51]

The total expulsion of Bani-Nader Jews in Medina took place in the fourth year of Muhammad's migration to Medina around 626 a.d. Muhammad had succeeded in making Medina free of all Jews. The tribe of Khayber remained outside Medina and was given a choice to convert to Islam or face expulsion.

No treaty was actually honored by either side. Both Muslims and Jews had extreme mistrust in the other. What is evident is that this same mistrust is present in our modern times, over 1,400 years after Muhammad's death. It is indisputable that Muhammad wrote into the Koran the theology of killing the non-believers, and so we question how trust will ever be possible. Road maps to peace, throughout history, have consistently failed.

We ask rhetorically, if Allah does not like treacherous people, isn't beheading, by any moral standard, treachery? Does Allah approve those who behead others? Aren't stealing, robbing and murdering also, by any moral standard, treachery? Can Allah approve those who steal, rob and kill? How about the treachery of persons who wage Jihads for material gain?

Does Allah condone one set of actions for the Muslim and one set for non-believers? Any reasonable person can see the double standard here.

One person committing a deed is treacherous, while the Muslim is not treacherous if he commits the same deed. In all other religions, truth applies to every one of God's created human beings. In Islam, Allah requires far less of the Muslim than he does of the non-Muslim. But the true God is no respecter of persons; His ways are perfect and holy and apply to everyone, even His prophets.

I acknowledge that the majority of Muslims yet are peaceful people. Whether this comes from the peaceful Muslim's personal ignorance of, or rejection of, the violence in the Koran, we do not know. But I give them the benefit of the doubt. What is undeniable, however, is that violence remains forever cemented in their holy books, and it cannot be ignored when we compare the theology to other religions.

Shortly before his death, Muhammad received an Orthodox Christian delegation from Najran to discuss matters of the faith with him. The Christians realized Muhammad's strength, and perhaps they hoped to establish for themselves a treaty whereby they could practice their faith freely.

Only at this late date did Muhammad come to realize what Christians believed and did not believe. Muhammad's final rejection of Christianity was evident when he announced, "And whoever seeks a religion other than Islam, it will never be accepted of him, and in the hereafter, he will be one of the losers" (Koran 3:85).

Muhammad's attitude against all non-believers is recorded in four discourses. The first discourse (vv. 1–32) was probably revealed soon after the Battle of Badr. The second discourse (vv. 33–63) was revealed in 9 A.H. on the occasion of the visit of the Christians of Najran. The third discourse (vv. 64–120) appears to have been revealed immediately after the first one. The fourth discourse (vv. 121–200) was revealed after the Battle of Uhud.[52] These discourses are but another example of the evolution of Muhammad's doctrinal perceptions about Christianity and Judaism. The shift of his understanding of these two faiths takes place in the departure from earlier understandings in the Koran where the God of the Jews and Christians are one and the same as the God of Muslims (Koran 21:108).

The tactics of Islamic organizations and Muslim apologists in the West is to replicate, when they are minority, Muhammad's early life in their approach to Christians and Jews. They answer quickly that "We believe in

Jesus Christ as a prophet," and, "There is no compulsion in religion." They may even concede freedom of conscience when they say, "I worship that which you worship not, and you worship that which I worship not, to you your faith and to me mine."

Although we do not detract from any genuine attempt(s) by Muslim organizations that seek to sincerely serve their own people, we do not see any fruit being borne in dialogue with Muslims, unless both Muslims and non-Muslims bear the *same respect and theological open-mindedness* towards each other. Every attempt will be futile if it does not deal with the theological roots of the others' faiths. The theology is found in the holy books, and cannot be reduced to what the adherents claim as the faith, apart from those books. This is the only reliable common ground for meaningful dialogue.

Furthermore, as Muslim voices cry out demanding rights in the Western world, we should raise an equal or greater cry about the lack of rights the citizens of their countries truly have. Muslim fanatics will grasp every single opportunity for more protection of their agenda here, but we should likewise charge them with neglect of their countrymen left at home. CAIR, for example, is quick to point out any hint of denigration of Islam in the West, but it says nothing about the denigration of other faiths in Muslim countries. It does little to speak up about vociferous calls for the deaths of Jews and Christians at the hands of Muslims.

We must never forget those Christians and Jews still living in Muslim countries. Their right to worship according to their conscience, their freedom of assembly, and their prohibition to evangelize the society in which they live all should enter the discussion as valid talking points. Islamic organizations should be the first ones to call for the rights of persons within their native countries, and their power and influence should be exerted within those Islamic countries to assure us that what they seek here is not a repeat of what exists there.

Muslims, Christians, and Jews in the West should pressure Islamic organizations toward moderation. All persons of faith must support the freedom of conscience, and require Muslims to adhere to the Islamic tenet that there is no compulsion in religion. Muslims enjoy living in free societies, but they should seek the right to investigate other faiths as part of their God-given rights. America is a model for differing peoples to live in harmony, side-by-side. Muslims in the West now need to lead by example, and challenge the fanatical hard-liners *through learning what the Koran itself really says.*

When Muslims in the West are invited to come into a church to "teach" about Islam, we should require a reciprocal right to go into the Mosques and "teach" about Christianity. Equal opportunity should be given to all faiths in any inter-religious dialogue, and we have allowed ourselves to remain far from asking for reciprocation and an equal opportunity to preach our views to them.

THE SON OF PROMISE: ISAAC OR ISHMAEL?

Abraham (Ibrahim in Arabic) and Ishmael (Ismael) are crucial figures in the Islamic faith. All of Islam is based on unsupported claims attached to Abraham. We examine three major claims attached to Abraham.

THE FIRST CLAIM: ABRAHAM WAS THE FIRST MUSLIM

The linguistic term "Muslim" was in use before the time of Muhammad, and it always meant "a person who submits to the will of Allah." The use of the term has dramatically changed since the appearance of Islam in 610 a.d. Muhammad redefined it to designate persons who submit to the will of Allah; who believe in Muhammad as his final, most perfect prophet; and who believe in the Islamic doctrines.

It cannot be the case that Abraham was Muslim in the redefined sense, since Abraham lived long before. So Muhammad uses the term in two different ways. It applies in the limited sense to Abraham. When Muslims claim that Abraham was the first Muslim, they imply that Abraham was the first one to believe in Allah as he reveals himself in the Koran. Muslims also say that Adam and Noah also believed in the same Allah as he revealed himself in the Koran. "The same religion he has established for you as that he enjoined on Noah."[53]

Muhammad and his followers used the term "Muslim" (it in its expanded meaning) to refer to his new religious adherents. They must believe that he was their final prophet, etc. Yet, Muhammad and his followers *refuse* to use the term in the limited sense for Christians and Jews, and any other faithful people who follow the one true God. This is nothing more than the *wholesale stealing of the prophets from other religions* and inserting them into his. Now the ONLY faithful people have to be of the Islamic religion!

Abraham is said to be the first one who initiated the term "Muslim" and called those who followed to worship the one Allah as Muslims. "And strive in his cause as you ought to strive. He has chosen you and imposed no difficulties on you in religion. It is the cult of your father Abraham, and it is he who has named you Muslims."[54] Furthermore, Abraham is quoted as saying to his offspring not to die unless you are a Muslim.[55]

The major problem with this notion is, if Abraham was the first Muslim to know and worship Allah, and he initiated the term, what about Noah and Adam? Did they worship someone other than Allah?

In addition, Muhammad, in his Ahadith, states that the best religion is the religion of Abraham. "I do not know any other religion except Hanif." When he was asked what Hanif meant, Muhammad responded, "Hanif is the religion of Abraham; he was neither Jew nor Christian, and he used to worship none, but Allah."[56]

Adam and Noah are prophets in Islam, but it is unclear if they knew the religion or even worshipped Allah in the same way that Abraham is said to have worshipped him.

THE SECOND CLAIM: ISHMAEL WAS THE PROMISED SON

Muslims believe that Ishmael was the promised son, though the Koran does not say so. In Muhammad's Traditions, there is mention of both Isaac and Ishmael as sons of the Promise. Earlier Muslim commentators did not understand the implications of which son was the miracle son of Abraham, and so it was not much discussed until the 20th century, when Islam met with the West.

God blinded Muhammad such that he did not understand the Covenant God had made with the Abraham through Isaac, and so the Koran and Traditions leave the case wide open. Muslims cannot at all prove from their books that Ishmael was the Son of Promise; nor was Ishmael the miracle son who was offered up in sacrifice.

THE SON OF THE PROMISE

Abraham lived in Ur, a city in the south of modern day Iraq. The Muslims say that he was wondering about the fruitlessness of worshiping idols among his people during the rein of King Nimrod. His father, according to Islamic historians, was in the business of making statues. Abraham wondered about these useless, lifeless idols and planned in his heart to make spectacles of them and show his people how useless they were. Thus he broke all the statues of his people one night. (This shows a tendency on the historians' part to project Muhammad's personality back onto Abraham. Muhammad continuously tried to establish parallels between other prophets and his own life.)

The people of the city woke up to see that someone had smashed their gods, and it did not take long to decide Abraham was responsible for the act. Upon the king's order they set a fire, ready to burn Abraham at the stake. Abraham took off and left Ur.

Abraham cried out to Allah in Ur to grant him a son. "O, my Lord, grant me a righteous son. So we gave him the good news of a wise son."[57] This was, according to some Islamic historians, before his marriage to Sarah. But our next quote shows that his wife was standing nearby; this time he received the promise as he entertained angelic beings. "His wife, who was standing by, laughed. We bade her rejoice in Isaac and in Jacob after Isaac."[58] Regardless of whether Abraham received the promise once or twice, he received that it would come through Sarah, his wife, in Isaac and Jacob.

Hagar came to serve as Sarah's handmaid when they were in Egypt. Hagar was not even born when Abraham was still in Ur in Iraq. In Islam, slaves do not inherit, and Hagar was a slave of Abraham's. So she would not have been the one through whom the promised son would come.

The question of which son was offered up by Abraham was answered by Muhammad in the Koran. Many Muslim historians agree with Muhammad, as does Al-Tabari on page 158 of the first volume of *Tarih Al-Tabari* (The History of Al-Tabari). He says, "The past scholars differed as to who, among Abraham's sons, was offered as a sacrifice. Some say it was Isaac, others say it was Ishmael. Both variations been quoted from our prophet [Muhammad], but the proof for this is in the Koran, confirming what the prophet [Muhammad] already said that, Isaac, is the right version." But Muslim apologists today, who claim it was Ishmael, think they know better than Muhammad, at least on this point!

THE MIRACLE SON

Modern day Muslims believe, falsely, that Ishmael was the son of the sacrifice. They also think that Ishmael was, therefore, the miracle son. A grown man could sleep with a woman and make her pregnant, regardless of how old he was. Hagar was in her twenties when Abraham slept with her. He was in his late seventies, according to Islamic historians, and even older, according to the Bible. Where is the miracle in a young woman having a son? But, according to the Koran, Sarah was in her seventies when she conceived Isaac. When Isaac was born, the Bible records that she was over ninety, and Abraham was nearly one hundred years old. This is clearly evidence of God's miraculous birth through Sarah and of the fulfillment of His promise to Abraham.

THE THIRD CLAIM: ABRAHAM AND ISHMAEL BUILT THE BLACK STONE IN MECCA

Mecca, the holiest shrine for the Muslims and the site of the annual pilgrimage, is said to be the site of an ancient altar built by Noah and improved upon by Abraham and his son Ishmael. They say Abraham and his son Ishmael built the altar as a place of worship to the one eternal Allah! There is no record in history when this actual black square that exists today first appeared.

The Koran and Muhammad's Tradition give no substantiation to the claim that either Noah or Abraham had anything to do with its arrival on the scene. There is nothing in the Koran that tells us of a black stone, cube, or anything like what is there in Mecca today. No archaeologist has ever traveled there to carbon date the stone, and thus, who built it remains a mystery.

When Sarah asked Abraham to cast out Hagar and Ishmael from the home, the Koran suggests that Abraham took them close to Mecca. Abraham is said to have cried in Mecca,

> Lord, make this [Mecca] a land of safety. Preserve me and my descendants from serving idols. Lord, many they have led astray. He that follows me shall become my brother, but if anyone turns against me, you are surely forgiving and merciful.

Lord, I have settled some of my offspring in a barren valley near your sacred house so that they may observe true worship. Put in the hearts of men kindness towards them, and provide them with earth's fruits, so that they may give thanks. Lord: You have knowledge of all that we hide and all that we reveal; nothing on earth or in heaven is hidden from God. Praise be to God who has given me Ishmael and Isaac in my old age! All prayers are heard by Him . . . [59]

The text above indicates there was already a house of worship built there; the nature of worship in that house is unclear. Some Muslim historians claim that either Noah or Adam built that house. Jalaluddin Ahmed Alseyoti, in his commentary on Koran 14:37, says, " . . . that the reference to the 'House of God' was there [Mecca] before the flood of Noah."

What is the source for his certainty that this was built by Noah? If Noah built it before the flood, or Adam built it, how did it survive the flood? The house was built of clay, which would be dissolved in flooding water, so this supposition cannot be true at all.

If Mecca were as important to Abraham as Muslims say, why didn't he choose to live and die there? All Muslims agree that he is buried in Hebron, which is part of Israel today. The combinations of contradictions within the Koran and Muhammad's Traditions as to how important Mecca was to Abraham and Ishmael simply are not borne out by their burial ground being elsewhere. In general, there is so much confusion on any one point in Islam that we have to ask if the Koran is a true revelation from God or not. God cannot be the source of confusion, since He is light and truth and in Him there is no contradiction.

PROPHETS IN ISLAM

Muhammad earlier had said that all prophets come from the House of Israel. He did not perform any miracles, and had little understanding of Judaism. The Jews repeatedly asked Muhammad about doctrine, particularly about the Holy Spirit, and he failed miserably in his understanding of the Holy Spirit and other doctrines. If they took him at his early word that all prophets came from the House of Israel, they had to reject him based on his own proclamation, since Muhammad was *not* of Jewish descent. If they were to overlook this, Muhammad still failed to present clear doctrines, and did not offer a richer and deeper look at Who God Is.

So, how did Muhammad adjust to this? He added even more concepts in Islam, hoping to show that his revelation was a superior one to both that of the Jews and the Christians. As a result, there are many contradictions, and irreconcilable perspectives of prophets in the Koran and Muhammad's Tradition. So many opposing views are presented in the Koran that just about anyone could find something to agree with, and something else to vehemently disagree with. As a poor soul, was I destined to flip-flop through doctrines, shuffling theology around for my entire life? I sought the consistency that comes with truth. Muhammad's actions were speaking louder than his words, and the inconsistency his life leaves for the Muslim is a cause of many divisions in Islam today.

ALLAH SENT A PROPHET FOR EACH NATION

In Islamic writings, there are both prophets (Nabi) and messengers (Rasul). There is no clear distinction between the two, though it is said that not all messengers are prophets but all prophets are messengers. According to Muhammad, messengers cannot see the angels, while prophets do; all prophets are brothers, but not all messengers are. So we get the sense that a messenger is one-step down from a prophet.

According to some Muslim historians, there were 144 prophets sent by Allah to geographically scattered humanity. Not all of these prophets are named in the Koran, but only 25 of them. 17 prophets were selected from the Torah and the Psalms (which comprise the Islamic version of the Old Testament). Three prophets were selected from the Injil (the Islamic canon of a "Gospel" given to Jesus by Allah). Three prophets from Arab ancestry were also selected, adding Muhammad as the final prophet to the list of 25.

The Koran often repeats, "For every nation, there is a prophet."[60] These prophets spoke to their nations the real and final revelation found in the Koran in their own native language.[61] The Koran here, again, is self-contradictory, since it also claims elsewhere that prophets came from the lineage of the Jews. "We gave the Book to the Israelites and bestowed on them wisdom and prophethood."[62] Revelation and prophets come from the Jews alone, since the next text clearly states,

> Say: We believe in Allah, and in what has been revealed to us and what was revealed to Abraham, Ishmael, Isaac, Jacob, and the Tribes,[63] and in [the Books] given to Moses, Jesus, and the prophets, from their Lord: We make no distinction between one and another among them, and to Allah do we bow our will [in Islam.]. (Koran 3:84)

Christians must emphasize these points in their approach to Muslims, though to the Western mind they may not seem cataclysmic. To the Muslim, this is a troubling thread that may unravel his foundational beliefs in the Koran. We should ask them how they could reconcile the above three scenarios in the light of:

1. The Koran is a book revealed by Allah. "The Koran is such that it cannot be produced by other than Allah."[64]

2. Judeo-Christian theology states that God cannot be the source of confusion or contradiction. "This is the book. In it is guidance for all, without any doubt."[65]

3. Muhammad and three other prophets were Arabs, but the Koran, in 45:16, states that ALL prophets must come from the Jews. "We said aforetime, 'Grant to the children of Israel the Book, the power of command, and prophethood.'"

Allah has sent a prophet to the Japanese, the Chinese, the Dutch, etc. Maybe even the native Indians in America had one, but he is not known. Actually, there were so many different Indian tribes and tongues that maybe 40 were needed to serve this group alone. There are far more than 144 nations in the United Nations, so we can see how many different prophets would have been needed to follow this line of reasoning.

There were far more than 144 people groups throughout history by the time Muhammad delivered the Koran. And Muhammad says many of them were sent to Israel, so this leaves out a significant number of other people altogether. Are we to believe that all of these people groups changed their "revelation" of Islam and conspired to eliminate Muhammad's name so that when Muhammad arrived, there was no testimony predicting he would come that remained on the earth? Are we to believe that only Muhammad was able to deliver (and the Arabs after him to preserve) the Koran in its clarity?

ALL PROPHETS WERE SINLESS

In Islam there are two sects with their own concepts of sinlessness. One is found among the Shiites and the other among the Sunnis. Neither concept has widespread theological support among Muslims.

Shiites believe that the 12 Imams, who are said to be direct physical descendents of Muhammad, are all sinless, and therefore, infallible; that is, infallible in their teaching and in their personal conduct. There are many differences among the various Shiites' schools about sinlessness, and the Sunnis believe in an entirely different way; the same concept, but only among the prophets. The sources of faith for Sunnis, aside from lip service, do not include any of the Shiite twelve Imams.[66]

The general position taken by Islamic scholars is that the concept of Esam is the product of the 10th Century a.d. This means the concept arose in the third century of Islam,

well after Muhammad's death. Muhammad did not claim to be sinless, and the Koran identifies only Jesus Christ and His mother Mary as sinless. Esam linguistically means preservation or kept from, but when used in relation to religion, it can have a variety of meanings. The essence of its religious meaning is that the prophet is preserved from the stain of sin.

However, there are three major obstacles in Esam. The first question is whether or not it refers only to the prophet's beliefs as infallible, or whether or not it implies that his deeds also were sinless. The second question it raises is at what point the prophet was preserved from sin, i.e., at birth or when? I remind the reader here that Muslims do not believe an infant is born with original sin. Therefore, at what point was the prophet preserved from sin? Was he preserved from it as an adult? The third obstacle in this concept of Esam is never addressed by Muslim theologians: what is Allah's purpose in causing a prophet to be preserved of sin(s)?

Western scholars thought the concept of Esam has its origin in Jewish thought. D.M. Donaldson, Ignaz Gldezier, and Montgomery Watt, to mention a few, fail to credit Catholicism's huge impact on Islam, even though some reference is made to the Catholic doctrine of the infallibility of the popes. Though this Catholic dogma received its official stamp only in the late 19th Century, the belief was widespread for centuries.

> The Catholics claim that infallibility belongs in a special way to the Pope as the head of the Bishops ... [they cite Matthew 16:17–19 and John 21:15–17]. Christ instructed the Church to preach everything he taught (Matt. 28:19–20) and promised the protection of the Holy Spirit to 'guide you into all the truth' (John 16:13). That mandate and that promise guarantee the Church will never fall away from his teachings (Matt. 16:18, 1 Tim. 3:15) even if individual Catholics might.[67]

Catholics do NOT believe the Pope speaks infallibly because he is sinless; they claim he is a sinner like everyone else. Speaking on matters of faith and morals, the Pope is said to speak infallibly, because Jesus gave the guarantee of the Holy Spirit to the Church.

However, some Shiites believe that their Imams are sinless, and from this sinlessness comes their infallible speech. Other Shiites may have been influenced to believe that their Imams speak infallibly on doctrine due to Catholic influence. For Sunnis, infallibility ended with the death of the final prophet, Muhammad.

It needs to be underscored here that the ONLY prophet, according to the Koran, who was sinless was Jesus. Jesus Christ shines above all the others precisely because He was without sin. It was the desire of later Shiite Muslims to attribute such sinlessness to their Imams, most probably, in an effort to compete with Christianity. But, all of the Muslims show *no understanding* of what the claim means—that Jesus was without sin. They do not realize that He was the only one capable of propitiation,[68] or dying in our place!

The Judeo-Christian influences upon Muhammad, whether acknowledged or not, will have little impact in our discussions. Muslim theologians vehemently deny any hint that their religion was influenced by "foreign" elements. They simply say that the people of the book had *SOME* truths still left in their books, and thus there is some similarity. They continue that only the Koran contains *ALL* the truth. They do not dream that anything in conflict with the Koran could be true. Muslims believe that anything outside Islam is not true, since the Koran's meanings, visible or hidden, are all that is needed for life here on earth and hereafter. I might point out to the reader here a great difference. The Bible asserts that if it were to reveal all the Truth of God, it would require volumes bigger than all the earth could contain.

Neither the Koran nor Muhammad's Traditions declare that any prophet is sinless, with the exception of Jesus. However, Islamic scholars require the belief in all of the prophets as one of the principles in the Fourth Article of the Islamic faith. How did Islamic scholars come to believe that all of the prophets and Imams are sinless? *Muhammad would have said so if it were revelation.* Could we say that Islamic scholars are unaware of the gravity of their claims? How do they dare to add to Muhammad's words and add weighty concepts that are not in the Koran or Muhammad's Traditions?

Islamic theology did not assert sinless prophets until late in its history. But the revelation of the Koran is not open to additions and changes! This is its great claim. The revelation

should have ended with Muhammad. Esam is believed only by the most Orthodox of Muslims. Perhaps centuries later they painted the concept of a sinless prophet onto their own, much like the emperor's clothes.

The major reason, we believe, that Esam was *adopted into Islam* was to combat what was already written in the Koran about Jesus Christ and Mary, i.e., that they were the only sinless people. "Satan touches [makes unclean] every son of Adam on the day when his mother gives birth to him with the exception of Mary and her Son, Jesus Christ."[69] *Perhaps Esam was introduced so that Muslims would stop doubting their own holy books.*

Now, in recent centuries, we see that Orthodox Islam goes to elaborate lengths to prove that prophets were sinless, since they were elected by Allah to pass on His message to humanity. The prophets were needed to encourage the believers to be virtuous and faithful in worshiping Allah, and Allah would not choose hypocrites to convey his message! I can only sigh here. I find myself asking how long it will take for Al Qaeda followers to claim that Osama Bin Laden was sinless.

Allah reprimands hypocrites. "O you who believe, why do you say that which you do not do? Most hateful it is to Allah that you say that which you do not do" (Koran 61:2–3). "Do you conduct good practice on people and forget yourself?" (Koran 2:44). Muslims produce the argument that, since Allah obviously would not choose a hypocrite, the prophets must all have been sinless! They see no conflict with the Koran statement that only two were sinless—Jesus and Mary.

One of the fatal flaws in Islamic theology is attributing Adam's sin to forgetfulness. Adam is never mentioned as a prophet, though *he is regarded* as one. They have no problem saying that *all* the prophets were sinless, even though everyone knows Adam sinned. "And certainly we gave a commandment to Adam before, but he forgot; and we found in him no resolve" (Koran 20:115). If Adam, in fact, were found by Allah to have no resolve, then that leads to *highly unacceptable* notions.

Isn't Allah here blamed by scholars, when they say he did not give Adam enough faculties to follow the command? What kind of Allah would cast him, Eve, and the rest of humanity from the Garden of Eden over a mistake of forgetfulness? (Koran 2:36). Allah apparently favored Muhammad over Adam, giving Muhammad special treatment. "By decree shall we teach you to declare, so that you shall not forget" (Koran 87:6). Furthermore, the Koran states that the creation of Adam was imperfect, as he was created to toil and struggle (Koran 90:4 and 84:6).

Would Muslims accept labeling Allah with imperfections? NO! This would be blasphemy. But don't jump to conclusions yet. There was a verse that compensates, saying that Allah perfected Adam's creation (Koran 95:4). Now, which do we believe? That Adam was created imperfect, with no resolve, or that he was created perfect? It does not seem to matter to Muslims that they have it both ways.

All of the prophets in the Koran, with the exception of Jesus Christ, asked Allah for pardon and forgiveness. "Istighfar is the asking for forgiveness of sins,"[70] and "dhanb" is generally translated as sin. It means either a "sin, or a crime or a fault,"[71] and Khata' is a mistake, though sometimes an unintentional one.

Adam, in Koran 2:37 and 20:122, repents of his transgressions against Allah and himself using the word Ta'ba only when his nakedness is apparent to him (after he sinned). "Then they both ate of the tree and so their private parts became manifest to them and they began to cover themselves with the leaves of the Paradise for their covering. Thus Adam disobeyed his Lord and so he went astray" (Koran 20:121).

"They were clothed in the garb of innocence and knew no evil; now when disobedience to Allah sullied their soul and tore off the garment of their innocence, their sullied self appeared to them in all its nakedness and ugliness."[72] This is clear disobedience, with grave consequences that followed, and the sin cannot be dismissed as "forgetfulness."

It should be clear to the reader by now that Muhammad never heard the Good News, the Gospel of Jesus Christ. If he had, he may have become one of the great saints of the Christian world. But instead, he had discussions with Christians and Jews in his youth, in the marketplace, and he relied on the bits and pieces he heard to determine what those faiths were. He could never have heard the true and saving Gospel, as is obvious from the wrong claims about Christian beliefs in the Koran.

Every believer in Christ should take Jesus' Great Commission seriously. By proclaiming the Gospel, we might save the world from another Hitler or win a soul like Muhammad. It is said that Nikita Khrushchev memorized the entire New Testament in his youth but perhaps never saw a Christian live the abundant life, so he considered it rubbish and became an atheist.

MUSLIMS MUST BELIEVE IN ALL PROPHETS

The belief in all prophets is *MANDATORY* in Islam, and it is posted as one of the six Articles of the Islamic faith.

How can Muslims say they believe in a prophet but refuse to hear what that prophet said? I myself have tried to tell a Muslim I do not, as a Christian, believe that Mary is the third person in the Trinity, but they insist that I do because the Koran says so. They are obligated to believe in Jesus, but there is only one they are to follow by example: Muhammad. To claim to believe in someone but deny all that he taught makes no sense. This makes the use of the term "believe" a meaningless uttering. They believe differently in all the prophets before Muhammad than they do in Muhammad. This means they misuse the term "believe" among so many other terms. It is crucial to point out their use of terms and the different ways they apply those terms in their speech.

EZEKIEL IS ALSO A PROPHET

While Muslims "believe" only in the first five books of the Old Testament and the Psalms of David, they claim that Ezekiel was a prophet, though he came thousand of years after Moses and is not in the first five books of Moses, nor in the Psalms.

I began to realize that the priest who gave me the book on Christian martyrs knew very well what he was doing. May I thank him one day in Heaven! God planned his actions perfectly and masterfully tailored them for me.

I might mention here that St. Francis of Assisi knew that Christians had been challenged by Muhammad centuries before, and the Christians had failed to allow God to produce a miracle in front of Muhammad. St. Francis repented that the prophet had never had the chance to see whose God was real, so he set out to renew the challenge for the Muslims of his day. Francis was brimming with hope that the differences between Muslims and Christians could be resolved and many be won to Christ, if he could call upon God as did Elijah, in their midst. The Muslims loved his zeal but refused the challenge. However, he was loved by Muslims and welcomed to witness wherever he went. So would we be if we were filled with such holy zeal!

Christians did not wage war against Muhammad, but they did not succeed through pacifism to stop Muhammad from threatening them and ultimately warring against them.[73] Catholics have been trying pacifism for centuries, and many evil tyrants have succeeded with their acquiescence. It is no less today with the cries from the Catholic Church that we never should have gone to war in Iraq. It is WRONG to leave anyone to die without ever having heard the Gospel of Jesus Christ.

Catholics love to quote St. Francis when they say, "Share the Gospel, and, if necessary, use words." I lived among Catholics in the US for years and never once did I know they were Christian. This is a shame and is actually disobedience to Christ's Great Commission. If GOD does not have our zeal, then certainly we have other gods before him that do receive our zeal.

THE ISLAMIC CLAIM THAT THE BIBLE IS CORRUPTED

Muslims believe that the Bible was corrupted and changed by Christians and Jews. It would have taken literally thousands of scribes and holy men scattered around the world to conspire to change every one of the extant versions. It would have required a level of cooperation that is not even possible in modern times with modern technology! We cannot even get every person who has access to nuclear weapons to agree to eliminate them. How much more so for deleting Muhammad's name from ancient manuscripts!

Yet, as a Muslim youth, I bought into this claim. It conveniently allowed me not to prove what was true. I did not ever need to read the Bible as long as I believed men wrote it. The Bible, I thought, might be as full of contradictions as was the Koran, which speaks of itself as the dictated word of Allah.

Islamic scholars bear responsibility for discouraging billions of Muslims from ever opening a Bible, or trusting what a believer of another faith may say about his faith.

The Koran contains texts that contradict the Old and New Testaments, and when the scholars are faced with answering these contradictions, they resort to claiming that the Bible must have been corrupted from its original form.

It was an outright, expedient lie for Muhammad to begin to claim that Jews and Christians "corrupted" their own holy books. His motivation in the lie was self-serving; he could convince the ignorant that there were prophecies given in history mentioning him by name. He lied about the people of the book, to say that they plotted to hide verses that prophesied that Muhammad would be coming after Jesus. This elevated his own status as a prophet, answered the question why he was not foretold in their books, and gave Muslims, who hated the Jews and Christians, cause to ignore their religions forever.

Not only are the claims of the Bible verifiable historically, but the archaeological scrutiny and sequence of historical events recorded in the Bible has proven its veracity to date.

With a minimum of two audiences here, Muslims and Christians, I hope to be more than fair in examining the claims of the Koran, and I would hope that the Muslim readers would be more than fair in examining and studying the Bible.

JEWS AND CHRISTIANS DID NOT ALTER THE SCRIPTURES

The best-known translation in America of the Koran is *The Meaning of the Holy Koran*, by Abdulla Yusuf Ali. Mr. Ali declares,

> The correct translation of the Tawrah [Torah] is therefore "The Law." In its original form, it was promulgated by Moses, and is recognized in Islam as having been an inspired Book. But it was "lost" before Islam was preached. What passed as "The Law" with the Jews in the Prophet's[74] time was the mass of traditional writing.[75]

Mr. Ali makes his stand even more direct: "The Tawrah mentioned in the Koran is not the Old Testament as we have it: nor even the Pentateuch."[76] How convenient it is for the Koran to re-define other religions' Holy Scriptures! What a theological coup.

The Psalms of David fare no better than the Torah as Mr. Ali's sweeping proclamations continue.

> David's distinction was the Psalms, which are still extant. Though their present form may possibly be different from the original and do undoubtedly include Psalms not written by David, the collection contains much devotional poetry of high order.[77]

The Muslims take liberties with others' religions that they disallow for their own. To make similar claims about the Koran would be called blasphemy. Is this not the height and perfection of arrogance?

Mr. Ali believes also that

> The Injil (Greek, Evangel=Gospel) spoken of in the Koran is *not the New Testament*. It is *not the four Gospels* now received as canonical. It is the single Gospel which, Islam teaches, was revealed to Jesus, and it matches the Koran, which the Muslim claims Jesus taught. Fragments of this Injil survive in the Bible as we know it, but other traces survive in the Gospel of Childhood or the Nativity, the Gospel of St. Barnabas, etc.[78]

Mr Ali did not enlighten us how he knows the Bible is a fabrication. The original no longer exists, according to him, so how can he know which fragments of it remain? He says only that which agrees with the Koran is from the original Gospels and Torah. The Koran refers to the people of the book as knowing the truth, and it is these who are to be sought for knowledge.

The apologists cite,

> [Allah] has made plain to you the religion that he enjoined upon Nuh [Noah] and that which we have revealed to you and that which we enjoined upon Ibrahim [Abraham] and Musa [Moses] and Issa [Jesus] that keep to obedience and be not divided therein; hard to the unbelievers is that which you call them to; Allah chooses for himself whom he pleases, and guides to himself him who turns [to him] frequently.[79]

As we stated above, the Koran "recognizes" only the first five books, called the Torah, along with the Book of Psalms from the Old Testament. But Muslims today do not even admit these are accurate. Instead, Muslims are the ones that change the ancient holy books! The theological coup, with all of its thefts, continues unabated.

The son of the Promise to Abraham was clearly Isaac, not Ishmael. Abraham thought it was Ishmael, but *God corrected him outright, saying it was Isaac through whom the blessing of God* would come. In Genesis 17, God says that His Covenant would be established with Isaac rather than Ishmael.[80] Muslims today claim their prophets are sinless, though the Koran is clear only Jesus was sinless. The Koran claims that Christians believe in three gods, but *this is not true*. Muslims ignore the Torah and claim *Ishmael was the one Abraham offered up to God*. The list of Biblical truths that have been modified, or changed outright in the Koran, can go on and on.

It is this mind-boggling double-speak in the Koran that claims the Torah is legitimate, but presents an opposite theology and narration of historical events. There are even places where the sister of Moses is confused with the Mother of Jesus. Can it be more obvious this is not Divine dictation?

It is noteworthy that, although Muslim scholars believe that the New Testament[81] is not authentic, they nevertheless quote from them, intensively using them as a whip for the Christians. Muslims feel superior by projecting their own theology's inadequacies onto others. They remain comfortable in the denial that Islam affords them. Muslim scholars find it *unnecessary to answer* when, or who, actually "corrupted" these ancient Scriptures ... *they simply believe it and that settles it.*

But we ask, since the only people who had access to the Scriptures for so many centuries were the very priests and holy men of the temples, why would such holy men change a single word? Why would anyone risk offending God by changing His Word? The Jews certainly revered God so much that they would not even write out the name of Yahweh in full. Even today, Jews reverently write out G-d rather than spell it out in full.

We have more original texts of the Bible than we do any other book in history. We have a relatively *small* number of copies of Homer's Iliad. Since this small number of copies of Homer's Iliad all agree, we accept that we know what Homer actually penned. Yet we have *thousands* of very early texts of the Bible, and all of them agree. But doubters even today prefer to think we do not know what the original texts were. Muhammad's outrageous lies and self-serving religious claims were but attempts to bolster his reputation, wealth and prominence, rather than deliver an authentic message from the One True and Holy God of Israel.

There simply was no time period in which Scripture would have been altered, since there were too many believers at any given time that would have been alarmed at such revisions! Geographically, and substantially, the corruption of the Bible never happened.

Christians and Jews did not change the Old Testament. No one changed the words of Jesus Christ to eliminate Muhammad's name. Jesus said there would come after Him many who would claim to be the one we should follow, but we are NOT to believe them. In fact, in the *very last verse* in the New Testament, on the last page of the book of Revelations, we see a harsh warning to anyone who would dare to change even a word of the Scripture. John, who was one of Jesus' youngest disciples, wrote this book. Every Christian alive at the time, and since, has not dared to change God's Word.

The earliest Jews in the wilderness saw God's Judgment come to those who worshipped with strange fire. They knew that those who grumbled against Moses died. They knew that those who violated God's Word and touched the Ark of the Covenant died immediately. With such drastic consequences in mind, Jews never would have altered their ancient texts, especially on something as important as a coming prophet. And if they altered their ancient Scriptures, wouldn't they have first deleted the lines that put them in a bad light? No, the truth is that they have never altered their Scriptures.

The same mandate exists for the Christians. The earliest disciples saw the Holy Spirit strike Ananias and Sapphira dead for lying to the Holy Spirit (in front of the other disciples) about selling their house.[82] They knew that Adam and Eve's sin was to disobey God's Word, and that Jesus had come and suffered a horrible death to redeem us from such sinful disobedience. They would never have deleted a prophecy given by Jesus about Muhammad coming, since *they lived and died by every word Jesus spoke. His words gave them life. They were worth dying for.* And, had they wanted to alter their Scriptures, they would have first deleted the mistakes of Peter, and they would have wanted to place themselves at the foot of the cross rather than let the world know they abandoned Him and fell down in their faith at times.

God, when He gives His Word through the inspiration of the Holy Spirit, is WELL CAPABLE of preserving that Word for all generations. To assert otherwise is to say

God had no interest in its dissemination and preservation.

Muslims sense that their Koran somehow does not stand up to other religions' holy books. The best hope they have to keep their followers intact is to spread lies about the other faiths. The claim that the Bible was corrupted is but one of the claims that Muslims employ to discredit the Bible. We have yet to see them answer rationally the claims of the Bible and their implications.

Some modern Muslim apologists show superficial understanding of how the Bible was consolidated into one book; they show similar ignorance regarding the Koran and how it was compiled. "Allah Himself guaranteed its preservation and that is why the whole of the Koran was written during the lifetime of the Prophet Muhammad."[83] Well, if they claim Allah was able to preserve the Koran, why do they say Allah was not able to preserve it earlier in the Jewish and Christian Scriptures?

A respected figure in Islamic theology in America, Seyyed Hossein Nasr, purports that Greek and Roman influence on Christianity was so extreme, that Christianity became "Hellenized." At the end of the Hellenization process, the Scriptures were "corrupted."

I will grant that early cults and followers of Christ chose to emphasize one theme over another, and magnified one aspect of Christ over another. But they did not *re-write* Scripture. The Catholic hierarchy has always claimed that the Church stands on two pillars, Sacred Scripture and Holy Tradition. The *liberties were taken with TRADITION*, and not with written Scripture. What the Catholic Church now sees as Tradition is basically what the Bishops and Popes through the ages have "discerned." Even though Catholics *do not read Scripture, they never altered it*. Some cults were indeed Hellenized in their practices and beliefs (sic), and in other cults, Christ was transformed almost into an "Aryan" solar hero for the Europeans.[84] *But they did not alter Scripture!*

The very reason the Scriptures were given to mankind is precisely so that each and every believer would NOT be subject to false shepherds. They would be able to recognize those who came preaching another god. God reveals Himself in the pages of Scripture, so that His people would know Him. God promised that He, Himself, would shepherd His sheep, and that is proved true through the reliability of His written Word.

An apologetic method employed by Muslims is to select verses that appear to contradict other verses in the Bible. The same few verses in Scripture used by Muslims over and over keep them blinded to any answers given by Christians. These seeming contradictions have been explained to them again and again, but they refuse to listen.

In all fairness, some of the verses that they cite are difficult to understand on the surface, and to the unbeliever, they seem to contradict other verses. None of the verses undermine or discredit the fundamentals of Jewish or Christian beliefs, nor the inspiration of the Holy Spirit that guarantees the Scriptures. There are postings on the Internet that I refer to for the reader. For the honest Muslim, with a sincere thirst for the truth, these same verses are not hard to understand, since the answers have been long-standing in Christian theology. Most Bible-reading Christians can answer their allegations.

In the Gospel, according to Matthew 4:5, Satan tempted the Lord Jesus Christ while He was in the wilderness. The New International Version states that the devil took the Lord to some high place. Muslims wonder, "How can the devil carry God?" To them, this is a blasphemy found in the Gospels. Satan offered Jesus Christ the world if He would bow down to him. They do not listen to Jesus' answer but explode in outrage, "How can the devil even dare such an audacity with God?"[85] But they find no such outrage that the Satanic verses appear in the Koran, yet all of it is called the word-for-word dictation of Allah.

For the Christian who does not read the Bible, these may seem difficult passages in the Scriptures. The Muslim does not believe in original sin, so how will he understand Jesus' fasting and being tempted but not sinning? How will he understand that the devil was given authority in the earth through Adam's fall, and that Satan did not know who Jesus really was until He was resurrected? If Satan knew that He was the Son of God, he would have fled, as did demons flee who *did* know who Jesus was. Jesus was able to clothe His Divinity with humanity, and that is why He came to His own, walked in this world, and the world knew Him not.

Muslims consider it their religious duty to inject doubts in the minds of Christians, in the hope of winning them as converts to Islam. Ignorant "Christians" do indeed convert to Islam, but not the ones who have known Jesus in His Glory. Would that we were as bold and as zealous as the Muslims in sharing our faith!

The reverse happens when a Christian goes to evangelize the Muslim armed with contradictions in the Koran. Unless the Christian believer has done his homework, he will only appear to be superficial in his understanding of the Koran. It takes some work, but it is to this end, the successful evangelization of Muslims, that I offer my testimony. May we go wisely educated, boldly with confidence, to share our faith in love.

False beliefs about Christianity are major stumbling blocks that prevent Muslims from seriously considering the authenticity of the Scripture. The matter worsens when Muslims go from one Protestant denomination to another, having to hear why the other denominations are "devil worshipping, tongue talkers" or that the others do not believe in the "gifts of the Spirit" or the full Gospel. For so many centuries, Muslims have heard what is wrong with the other Christians that they see a fragmented mirror of Christ in His sheep. One is told that he is baptized into Christ, but another comes and says that he must be re-baptized into that Church denomination, etc.

Muslims have their own "denominational" differences as well. In fact, from one Mullah to the next, one will find differing interpretations of the Koran. The Muslims lack one unified teaching perhaps even more than do the Christians, but they do not show this to the outsiders. They present a unified face for the sake of furthering Islam.

Protestant and Catholic have their share of scandals in the life of priests, bishops, cardinals, and even popes in the past. Muslims mistakenly see the Catholic Church as representing all of Christendom. The political correctness of the Vatican's proclamations

and its attempt to legitimize Islam is confusing the clear Gospel of Christ, mixing it with man's opinions. The Catholic Church wrongly holds that any religion is OK to bring a person to Heaven. It is NOT religion that brings a person to Heaven. Jesus said, "I am the way and the truth and the life. No one comes to the Father except through me" (John 14:6 NIV). The Catholics have so rationalized the *Logos of God* that they have gone full circle to believe that Christ can be found through all religions. In fact, Catholics target Protestants for conversion more than they do the Muslims. Their outreach is to the Protestants, who they see as more of a thorn in their side than Muslims.

Another objection Muslims raise, as well as Jews, is that the concept of the Trinity cannot be found anywhere in the Bible. They claim that this is a Christian "invention." But, if we look in the Old Testament itself, we find verses that state the Holy Spirit was the One who anointed David king. The same Spirit hovered above the waters in the book of Genesis and was there at the Creation.

The Holy Spirit anointed also David's predecessor, Saul, the first king of Israel. It was because of this anointing (and its Divine origin) that David would not kill Saul when he had the opportunity. Who was the fourth person that appeared in the fiery furnace with Meshach, Shadrach and Abednego, "Like unto the Son of God?" The Son of God has a Divine origin, does He not?

There are numerous prophecies in the Old Testament regarding a coming Messiah.

Isaiah 7:14 indicates a "virgin will give birth" to Immanuel, the Son of God. Isaiah 53 gives one of numerous prophecies describing His wounds, and the punishment He would take on for our sins. These prophecies were clearly fulfilled in the birth and subsequent death of Jesus on the cross. Psalm 22 records that they "cast lots for His garments."

I greatly paraphrase Josh McDowell when I say that he stated that, out of hundreds of Hebrew prophecies in the Bible, Jesus fulfilled nearly every one. McDowell writes on page 141 of *Evidence That Demands a Verdict*,

> The apostles throughout the NT appealed to two areas of the life of Jesus of Nazareth to establish His Messiahship. One was the resurrection, and the other was fulfilled messianic prophecy. The OT, written over a 1,000 year period, contains several hundred references to the coming Messiah. All of these were fulfilled in Jesus Christ, and they establish a solid confirmation of His credentials as the Messiah.

Our Jewish brethren, of course, disagree, citing over 3,000 years of Jewish interpretation of their own Scriptures, which conclude that no one has fulfilled the Messianic prophecies.

However, our position is that the Bible itself is proven to be true because of the overwhelming fulfillment of its predictive prophecies. Jesus

Christ's Second Coming will fulfill the remaining prophecies. In our estimation, the probability that any one person could fulfill this many prophecies in his lifetime mathematically approaches one in a million, to the hundredth power.

The Messiah is also the Kinsman-Redeemer. How can a mere mortal be a Redeemer unless he is of Divine Nature? Sinful man could never keep the Covenant, and we see time and again, though God worked miracle after miracle, and literally dwelt among them in the Tabernacle, they kept not their part of the Covenant and fell into worshipping other gods.

This is not to criticize the Jews, as do the Muslims. The Christian is well aware that he has his own sinful nature and could not have kept the Covenant either. This is why God promised that He would establish the New Covenant between Himself, and that man could be redeemed through what God would supply, namely, that Jesus Christ took our sins upon Himself and paid the price for all of us, captive to sin, to be set free and be reconciled to God.

The discovery of the "Dead Sea Scrolls" after World War II verified beyond anyone's doubt that the accuracy of the Holy Scriptures was recorded with utmost care and attention to every detail. In fact, Israel was so long in disclosing their contents, some say, because the Scrolls show that many Jews, at the time, accepted Jesus as the one prophesied, the Messiah, God's Son.

THE KORAN IS AUTHENTIC ONLY IN ARABIC

If the English speaking Christian quotes from the English translation of the Koran, a Muslim will resort to saying that he can trust only the original language of the Koran in Arabic. This is a cop-out. With the information provided in this book, you are very well armed. I have studied the verses in their original Arabic language rather than any other translation. Some verses are unmistakable in any language. For example, how many ways are there to translate "kill the infidel"?

In addition to the Koran and Ahdith Qudsiyais, which are both considered authoritative, is Muhammad's Tradition, or Ahadith[86] in Arabic. This is a series of writings said to be the actual words and deeds of Muhammad. According to historical data, Muhammad himself was unable to read or write. The Ahadith is said to have been spoken from the lips of Muhammad, and others transcribed it exactly as it was spoken. However,

transcribing the Koran took place approximately 200 to 400 years after the death of Muhammad in 632 a.d. by men who had never met Muhammad.

Muhammad's Hadith (Arabic for small tales, or legends) is of equal weight to the Koran, as Muhammad is said not to have spoken out of his own desires, but by Divine inspiration. "The fundamental teachings of Islam are based in the Koran and the Hadith,"[87] and as we shall presently see, both are claimed to be Divine in origin.

The Hadith is considered to be a clarification of the Koran, containing admonitions for practically living the Muslim faith.[88] "O people, understand my words, which I convey to you. I leave behind me two things, the Koran and my example, the Sunnah, and if you follow these you will never go astray."[89]

We have every reason to believe in the accuracy of Muhammad's Hadith, since most of the Middle Eastern civilizations have had long histories of oral traditions. Yet, again, how is it that Adam could forget one commandment from Allah while mere men could remember huge volumes? These oral traditions seem to be passed on from generation to generation in their entirety, unchanged, and have proven to supply us with historical events and data otherwise unrecorded.

THE NULLIFICATION THEORY

It became necessary in the exchange of ideas over the centuries for the Muslim scholars to develop a system for their adherents to maintain their faith in the face of logical and compelling apologetics by non-Muslims. Thus, whatever is difficult in the Koran is to be dealt with by the "nullification theory."

If we extend out the logic, we would have to say that when Allah revealed the Koran, he meant little or nothing in some early statements, since these were subject to many other opposing statements within the same "revelation." We might go so far as to say Allah had no obvious purpose in mind when he recited certain verses in the Koran to Muhammad, since, before he was finished, he said other things that only serve to confuse and cauterize man's attempts to understand Allah. The Muslim asserts that each and every statement in the Koran is attributable to Allah, and Allah does not have to make any sense in his "revelation." He can say whatever he pleases, true or false.

To allege that Allah has little consistency in adhering to the truth is to say that it is permissible for Allah to be a liar. This is a blasphemy, since Allah should not and would not deny his own words. The idea that Allah has no eternal, universal, unchanging principles is blasphemous. It would be outrageous for a flip-flopping Allah to demand more of humankind than he would of himself. Allah does ask the Muslim to be consistent in his faith, in his good deeds, and to show consistency in prayer, etc. Does Allah show greater consistency in the Koran?

The logical outcome of what the "nullification theory" asserts is unthinkable . . . that man is more consistent than Allah. It cannot be that man is more consistent than Allah, so the nullification theory is self-defeating. It hopes to glorify Allah, when it diminishes him beyond what any atheist could do.

Not only is man capable of being consistent, but nature itself is consistent. Scientists believe now that Jupiter, the largest planet in our solar system, was PULLED into the sun's orbit. It came from very far away, and without its intense gravitational pull, the earth would have been destroyed long ago by the barrage of meteors entering our solar system. If Jupiter's orbit were elliptical instead of circular, it would pull earth away from the sun. Everything in the universe reveals order, not contradiction. To claim that the Creator of all this *harmony and balance*, reveals *his true nature is inconsistent*, defies logic.

If we ask the Islamic theologian, "What verses have been nullified by Allah?" he gives the amazing explanation following: "Allah nullified the law of the verse, chapter, or book, yet he keeps its recitation by the believers valid." This means that even though Allah nullified an entire verse, or chapter of the Koran, he allows us to recite and quote it.

But another Islamic theologian says, in answer to us, "If a verse, chapter or book is nullified by Allah, its recitation is forbidden!" This would include something that is so obviously false and misleading to the faithful Muslim that it is not even allowed to be quoted from the Koran. The interpretation of "nullification" itself varies from theologian to theologian.

At first, this sounds absurd to the Western believer. Why keep verses and chapters which are said to be no longer valid? Is it because 2/3 of the Koran would be "nullified" with very little remaining? The Muslim would answer us with a smile, saying, "Oh, but it is still the word of Allah!"

The Muslims offer us rebuttal by saying, "Don't you Christians claim that some of the Old Covenant has been nullified by the New, such as animal sacrifices?" The answer we give here is, "No, these were not nullified sacrifices. They foreshadowed Jesus, the Lamb of God, who made the ultimate sacrifice for our sins. They pointed to who was to come in the future." Animal sacrifices were proscribed at a point in time when Israel was yet to receive the Messiah. The Messiah was also foreshadowed in the spotless lamb's blood over the Israelites' doors at Passover.

Adam and Eve covered themselves with leaves, but God brought them animal skins, which necessitated the shedding of blood by an animal. God says in Genesis that without the shedding of blood, there is no remission of sin. This is the justice aspect of God's holiness: He must satisfy the requirements of His justice. Jews received the forgiveness of their sins as they offered an unblemished, spotless sacrifice. Jesus is the one pure sacrifice, for all eternity, for any who desire to come to the Father. *His coming did not nullify the Law*; rather He demonstrated the fullness of the Law (love), and He fulfilled it.

The "nullification" spoken of in the Koran is of a totally different kind, where *there are moral directives changed, historical claims abandoned, and even names of prophets changed*. The Koran is "nullified" to get around glaring *contradictions in theology*. The truth of Judaism and Christianity is upheld in the Koran, but then the eternal truths get rescinded in the Koran. (One thing cannot be true at one time, and then not true later on. This is called relativism.) Lengthy discourses and verses within the Koran itself are nullified to reflect shifts in Muhammad's attitudes and changes in his theology.

The sheer number of contradictions within the pages of the Koran is staggering. Koran 2:62 reads, "Believers, Jews, Christians or Sabeans: whoever believes in God and the Last Day, and does what is right, shall be rewarded by their Lord; they have nothing to fear or regret." This text is unambiguous and does not take its meaning from its context. It confirms

(Allah is declaring) that devout Jews and Christians have no reason to fear that they could be following a false ideology.

If we ask the Muslims, "Must these devout Jews and Christians believe in Allah as revealed to Muhammad?" Isn't it sufficient for them to believe in Yahweh? Why would there be a need to "convert" the other peoples of the book? The Koran answers this in the very same book, 2:4: "And who believe in the revelation sent to you [Muhammad] and that which was sent before you [to the Jews and Christians], they have the assurance of [surviving] Judgment day [in Allah's favor]." This indicates that the Muslims *MUST also believe in the Old and New Covenant* in order to have the assurance of Judgment Day. The key word in this verse would be "AND."

It is a verse directed to the Muslim, not to the Jew or Christian, and the verse does not indicate that the Jews and Christians are obligated to believe in what came after their respective Revelations from God. Rather, the Muslims have the heavier of the duties to believe in all the Scriptures! As a matter of fact, believing in the previous books is within one of the six articles[90] of faith, which every Muslim must believe.

Muslim children are not taught analytical skills enabling them to investigate the Old and New Covenants, as the Koran commands and orders. Islam is most often passed along orally between generations, almost like a folk religion, with few Muslims ever actually reading (or learning the Arabic to read) the Koran.

Those verses, which encourage the Muslim to seek counsel from the adherents of Judaism and Christianity, are purposely left out of the oral teaching. Muslim nations find it threatening for the population to study other religions, and thus they discourage it, making Bibles and such completely unavailable (or illegal) to the public. Saudi Arabia, as well as many other Muslim nations, forbids Christians or Jews from even discussing their faith with a Muslim. Ignorance is looked upon as the friend of faith, rather than its enemy.

The Bible is generally dismissed by modern day Muslims as having been "corrupted," and no further inquiry takes place. There is tremendous peer pressure NOT to examine the tenets of others religion, though Allah says otherwise in the Koran. In fact, most modern day Muslims have no idea that the Koran states they are to investigate Christianity and Judaism (and believe in them). They would deny this appears in the Koran even if it were shown to them. If you opened the Koran for them, they might say you (or they) do not understand Arabic, anyway.

Unfortunately, to further hinder the light of Jesus Christ, Muslims are warned, under threat of death, that were they to "convert," they would be "apostate." There is in these threats the implication that the books are "different" religions, in contradiction to Islam, rather than the same religion of which the Koran claims to be the apex.

We imagine earlier civilizations, with less education, might be prohibited from studying Christianity and Judaism, with the excuse that they might be swayed to leave Islam. But today's Muslim populations have better access to education, and many can read and write. Are they allowed to explore other faiths? No; everything but Islam is forbidden.

The "threat to Islam" that Judeo-Christian troops in Saudi Arabia present was seen to be so imminent that US soldiers were forbidden to practice their own faith in the confines of the camps! This directive was imposed on Western "friends" who were there to "protect" the kingdom from invasion. These "friends" were not allowed to call on their God to assist them! Only the name of Allah can be invoked on Muslim soil. Then *why in the world, can't this same Allah protect them without the "infidels" providing protection?*

Koran 2:4 reads, "And, believe in what I have revealed to you [the Koran] confirming the revelation which is with you [the Old and New Testaments] and do not be the first to reject it."[91] The Koran tells all Muslims that "Our God and your God are one[92] and unto Him we surrender." Muslims wonder why Jews and Christians don't want to convert. From the Muslim's viewpoint, Jews and Christians have nothing to lose and everything to gain. [The answer whispered these days is that they are incorrigible infidels, and it is Allah's will that they be killed.]

If Jews, Christians and Muslims all worship the same God—are truly worshipping the same Allah—then why build a mosque on top of a Jewish temple, or bury a Christian church by erecting a mosque on top of its rubble? It should offend Allah to have his temple destroyed and his churches dishonored. So, why have Muslims consistently dishonored the people of the Book, their temples and churches? Because, in a pick-and-choose world, they cite, "If anyone desires a religion other than Islam, never will it be accepted from him" (Koran 3:85).

Perhaps these accounts, having been compiled a few hundred years after Muhammad, DO have different authors with differing motives. Each man claimed his writing was the true Koran, so they put the jumble all together and now have the problem of claiming it all to be of Divine origin. See Koran 2:41, and 2:89. Perhaps what is needed is for all Muslims scholars to get together and canonize which verses are actually valid and which are not, and then eliminate the ones that are invalid. After all, the Catholic Church held councils on true doctrine. But Muslims will never agree to this, or to any reform of Islam.

The Koran, minus the Hadith, remains unintelligible in many cases in the work-a-day life of man,"[93] but the obedience to Allah and His prophet is a requirement of Islam. "O you who believe . . . obey Allah and His Apostle" (Koran 8:45–46).

The majority of Muslim scholars and theologians believe that Jewish believers changed their own sacred Scriptures:

"Some of those who are Jews change words from their context."[94]

"Forgot a part of that whereof they were admonished"[95] [because they were motivated by personal gain, omitting "certain prophecies" in the Old Testament where "certain prophets" spoke about the coming of Muhammad or Ahmad].

The fact is, neither the Koran nor Muhammad's Tradition provide us with a single quotation as to where Muhammad's name was mentioned in the Old Testament. Jesus is altogether different: they refer to Isaiah 61:6: "And remember Jesus, the Son of Mary said, 'O, children of Israel! I am the Apostle of Allah to you, confirming the law before me, and giving glad tidings of an Apostle to come after me whose name shall be Ahmad.'" We cannot find this reference at all in the Bible, so they claim it was deleted.

In general, according to the Koran and Muhammad's Hadith, there are two classes of falsifications made by Jews and Christians:

1. Falsification of the text ("Tarif Al-Nas" in Arabic).
2. Falsification of the meanings ("Tahrif Al-Mainee").

But the Koran itself also states above that *neither the Old nor the New Testament were falsified in text or meaning.* "Do they not consider the Koran? Had it been from other than Allah they would surely have found therein much discrepancy" (Koran 4:82). It is literally baffling to see both points of view on any and every issue.

1. We, in summary, find Islamic claims that:
2. The Old and New Testaments are to be believed.
3. The Old and New Testament cannot be believed.
4. The revelation from Allah is the same in all three religions.
5. The three religions are irreconcilable.
6. Jews and Christians are believers.
7. Jews and Christians are unbelievers.
8. Jews and Christians will be in Hell.
9. Jews and Christians will be in Heaven.

Every Muslim is by necessity a "cafeteria" Muslim, since he must pick and choose which views are valid and which are not. It is unfortunate that MOST Muslims have never read their Koran. If they were to read it, they might find it cannot be the word of God.

MUSLIMS' CONFUSION ABOUT THE HOLY SPIRIT

Though I was one of the few who read the Koran and began to disbelieve it, I was still subject to its prejudices. The Islamic concept of the Holy Trinity turned me off to Christianity. I thought it was ridiculous that people could believe in three gods. But I had no choice but to read the early Christian writers, since they preceded Muhammad. I was not about to take the Koran at face value anymore; I already had plenty of doubts about Islam. I was thinking to myself, "If what the Koran says about Christians is true, I may as well read about Buddhism henceforth."

I read in Koran 6:101: "How can he have a son, when he has no wife?" I thought to myself, "This is sick that some people out there believe that God had a son! How could God have a son when he had no wife or maid? Surely God does not need wife nor a son, and why would he be in need if he is already perfect?" These were my questions then, and these are the same questions a majority of Muslims struggle with. In my humble opinion, if these are clarified for Muslims adequately, *they will desert Islam*.

My many years of experience with Muhammad's Tradition and classic Islamic commentators of the Koran proved to me that Muhammad thought of the son of God as a result of God having sexual relations. This seemed blasphemous to me. Now I know that Mormons also believe that God has sexual relations to populate planets. I guess some people can believe anything. But years after I found that this Muslim interpretation of Sonship was entirely carnal and worldly and did not at all represent what Christians were saying. Jesus was not born of a sexual relation between God and Mary. Even the Koran says that his mother Mary was a virgin and the Spirit of God Himself did not impregnate her by a man.

The Koran confuses the picture of Christians when it states in Koran 5:75 that

> The Messiah, son of Mary, was no other than a messenger, messengers (the like of whom) had passed away before him. And his mother was a saintly woman. And they both used to eat (earthly) food. See how we make the revelations clear for them, and see how they are turned away!

God, Jesus and Mary form the Christian "Trinity!" It was not enough for the Christians to have a God with a wife! Now we have a "Trinity" composed of a woman, son and God. This was just too much for my mind to accept. My search for the truth was compounded with lies about Christianity.

These were blasphemous concepts, and I thought to ask my next-door Christian neighbors why they believed things that infringed on God's holiness. I asked first my friend, who laughed. Subconsciously, I knew that no one could believe such rubbish, so I laughed as well. My friend then denied that Christians ever believed as the Koran claims, that Mary, Jesus and God form the "Trinity." I was temporarily relieved.

My friend's answer showed he thought he was helping me. He said, "No, that is not what we believe. It is what the Koran *claims* we believe." I just smiled. He confirmed my intuition that there was something seriously wrong with the Koran. In reality, his answer made the matter worse because he said, "The Trinity is composed of God the Father, God the Son, and God the Holy Spirit." Now I had brand new concepts to understand! First, Jesus is the Son of God, and secondly the Holy Spirit.

To solve the nature of Christ's Sonship, the priest and a Christian friend advised me to read Saint Thomas Aquinas's writings, although they warned me that this Aquinas writing was hard to understand. "I will understand it," I said to my advisors, riding high on my intellectual pride. I learned that the concept of generation is different with respect to God than in human beings, animals or plants, since God is true spiritual being.

Well, hallelujah! This was the first time I realized Muhammad did not grasp the nature of Jesus' Sonship. Furthermore, he did not understand with Whom the Trinity was composed. (I later realized that water comes in three forms: liquid, solid [ice], and vapor [clouds], yet it is not three different substances. In God, there is no difference in substance, but in appearance and form, yes. It was this understanding of the Trinity that helped me years later once I was saved.)

I was left to wonder about the Trinity. I also asked myself, why should God send His Son to save humanity? All we needed to do was repent, as the Koran dictates. What did we need to be saved *from*? If God sent His Son, did that imply that God's majesty was reduced or belittled? I had also to solve questions on the nature of Jesus Christ, and whether He is a savior or only a prophet, as Muslims claim. Adam's sin and its impact on humanity were also obstacles for me to overcome. Reading the Bible was the same as reading a piece of literature for me, since I was a Muslim. I did not yet have the light of the Holy Spirit to understand the Bible.

THE ANGEL GABRIEL

The angel Gabriel is said to have recited the Koran to Muhammad, but the angel is sometimes interchanged, in the Koran, with the Spirit of God or the Holy Spirit. We will look here at the concept of angels in the Koran and how this adds to the Muslim's confusion about the Trinity.

The mandatory belief in angels is one of the articles of Islamic faith.[96] "Whoever is an enemy to Allah and his angels and messengers, to Gabriel and Michael, Lo! Allah is an enemy to those who reject Faith."[97] This text declares that the angel Gabriel is a created being. Christians would agree with this. However, in Islam, this same angel is described as the Spirit of God (Koran 19:17).

"We sent to her Our Spirit, which appeared to her as a well shaped man." Elsewhere in the Koran, this same Spirit is called the trustworthy Spirit (al-Ruhul amin), or "the faithful Spirit"[98] (Koran 26:293). Yet we find in the Koran that this same Spirit is ALSO clearly identified as the Holy Spirit. "The Spirit of holiness [Holy Spirit] sent it down from your Lord with truth" (Koran 16:102).

Gabriel is but a created Angel (Koran 97:4) but is also described as God's Spirit

(Koran 19:17). Therein come down the angels and the Spirit, by Allah's permission in every errand." *Other angels are distinguished from God's Spirit, but not Gabriel.*

Muslims do not see any reason to seek to understand these distinctions more fully, since Allah can do whatever he pleases. Allah is written as both a creature and creator at the same time. This is the very premise upon which they deny the Divinity of Jesus Christ!

For all the trouble I had as a Muslim in first encountering the concept of the Trinity, I did not realize that the Koran mentions the Holy Spirit of Allah taking a created form in Gabriel! Here I was, a young Muslim, afraid of belittling or detracting from Allah's Majesty, while I could find *IN THE KORAN* the very concepts that I worried would "detract from" or "belittle" him. To add to my growing frustration, I read that Muhammad later on claimed to be the Holy Spirit. *This is something we know Lucifer would love to claim.*

The Holy Spirit, in the Koran, is said to have breathed into the Virgin Mary's body His Spirit, creating Jesus! "Mary, the daughter of Omran, who guarded her chastity and we breathed into her body of Our Spirit"[99] (Koran 66:12).[100]

The Muslim does not realize the claims in the Koran, about the Holy Spirit, present a picture of astonishing dimensions, in the following:

The angel Gabriel = the Spirit of God = the Holy Spirit = Muhammad = he who dwelt in Mary's womb, and became Jesus Christ.

In the equations made in the Koran, the temporal is equal to the eternal. Muhammad claimed in the Koran to be the Holy Spirit of God, but since this Spirit of God was breathed into Mary, did *he become Jesus?* No way. But this is what the Koran *ACTUALLY* says when all of the verses are collected.

CHRISTIAN CULTS ON JESUS CHRIST

The first three to four centuries after Christ's death and resurrection spawned as many Christian cults and theologies as there are 7–11 stores abundant in the US. The scope of this chapter is not to cover all these cults; the reader has access to them via the Internet or libraries. Rather I shall mention only one of the cults to indicate a parallel in their beliefs about Jesus with Islam.

The Muslim perspective of Jesus Christ is not unique to Islam. As a matter of fact, every Christian cult shared, to some degree, the Muslims' point of view on something. Mormonism, as I stated before, holds that the god of this world (Lucifer) had sexual relations in order to populate the earth. Islam says that Allah could have no son since he had no wife, implying that Allah would have to have sexual relations to have a son.

Muslims have two avenues to discover whether Islam is on shaky ground. The first is by studying the Koran, as I did, with a searching heart to know God, and studying Christian sources to see what the Christian actually believes. The second is to wait for a rude awaking on Judgment Day when he cannot appeal to God for another chance.

Tertulian, the Roman historian, spoke about the Abionites, a Christian cult in the second century b.c. He described their beliefs about Jesus as a noble man and a distinguished prophet since an angelic being lived in him. This basic misconception led them, as the case with Islam, to deny the divinity of Jesus and ascribe to him miracles mentioned only in non-canonical books as the Apocrypha of James and the Infancy of Joseph the Carpenter. The infancy Gospels claim that Jesus spoke from the moment of His birth, and for numerous such suppositions, they were never canonized into Scripture.

Justinian adds in his own writings that the Abionites believed Jesus was Divine by election and not by nature. That is to say Jesus began as the son of man but became the Son of God through His obedience.

It is prudent to remember that by the time Muhammad was born, in 570 a.d., the Catholic Church was well established in Rome, and no less than five councils had been held by the Church to determine correct doctrine. The Council of Nicea was held in 325 a.d. This was held specifically to the address the natures of Jesus. The Aryan heresy held that Jesus had been born a mere man but was "elected" to Divine Stature by God.

There was also the Council of Constantinople, in 381 a.d. that affirmed the final version of the Nicene Creed. Other heresies were banned in the Council of Ephesus, held in 431 a.d., the Council of Chalced, held twenty years later, in 451 a.d. Councils were almost always convened to establish distinctions between true doctrine and heresy.

The Eutyches Cult and the Monosophite Cult both held that Jesus had but one nature—human.

> The Nestorian heresy stressed the independence of the divine and human natures of Christ and, in effect, *suggested that they were two persons loosely united.* Nestorian communities lingered on in a few towns in Iraq but were concentrated mainly in Kurdistan, between the Tigris River and Lakes Van and Urmia, partly in Turkey and partly in Iran. In 1551, a number of Nestorians reunited with Rome and were called Chaldeans, the original Nestorians having been termed Assyrians.[101]

In 553 a.d., the Council of Constantinople II was held just before Muhammad's birth. There was a regular effort on the part of the Church to expel heretics, and thus many of the cults sought safety in the deserts of Arabia. It is only guesswork to imagine what Muhammad heard from the members of Christian sects and cults in the 7th Century. All that remain are the misconceptions we find in Islamic writings and the Koran itself.

JESUS WAS NOT LIKE ADAM

Muslims hope to disarm the Christian evangelist by immediately claiming, "But we honor Jesus. He was great prophet," or "Jesus was like Adam. Allah commanded him to be, and he was." What Muslims mean to say here is that Jesus was a creature like Adam! To say that Jesus was a creature, just a man, a prophet of honor, should not disarm or sway the Christian from proceeding. It should be an open door to speak about the nature of Christ as seen in the Koran. Since most Muslims have never read the Koran, Muslims are almost universally unaware of what the Koran really says.

Koran 3:59 reads, "Lo! The likeness of Jesus with Allah is as the likeness of Adam. He created him of dust; then He said unto him: Be! And he is." The dictated word of Allah proves that Jesus was NOT like Adam, as we see in these twelve ways:

1. Jesus was not created of dust, like Adam (Koran 66:12).

2. "And Mary, the daughter of Umran, who guarded her chastity and we breathed into her body our Spirit" (Koran 66:12). Jesus was born out of the Holy Spirit and came from the only virgin birth in history.

3. Who was the Father of Adam? Who was the Father of Jesus? We shall ask the answers from the Muslims themselves!

4. The mother of Jesus was Mary, a virgin, the Koran claims. Adam, on the other hand, had no mother.

5. Adam's sin is reflected in Muhammad's Hadith over and over again. "Adam forgot, and so do his offspring, and he sinned, and so do his offspring."[102]

6. Jesus was sinless, according to the Koran.

7. Adam died, both spiritually and physically, and returned to the dust. The Koran implies Jesus died and that He did *not* die. Muslims do not know which to believe.

8. Jesus is the Word, or *Logos* of God. Adam forgot the Word of God.

9. Jesus appears in the Koran with the destiny to return on Judgment Day to judge the world. Adam has the distinction of placing himself and all of his descendants under Judgment.

10. Adam married Eve and had children. Jesus did not marry or propagate children.

11. In the Koran, Adam asked forgiveness for his sin. Jesus had no sin.

12. Through Adam, all mankind experienced death and bondage to sin; through Jesus, all mankind can experience eternal life and liberty from sin.

The lengthy and detailed narratives on the person of Jesus both in the Koran and Muhammad's Tradition give clear testimony to the unique importance of Jesus Christ, not rivaled by Muhammad or any other prophets in Islam.

THE DIVINE NATURE OF JESUS CHRIST

I noticed how much time had been devoted to Jesus in Islamic theology. I asked myself what was so special about Jesus that the Koran had such emphasis on Him. I later came to understand that God bore witness to His Son in the Koran, sufficient to bring a curiosity about Him to all fair-minded Muslims.

The witness God placed in the Koran about Jesus is that He is called "The Word of God," "The Spirit of God," and "outstanding and near to God." Furthermore, he was born sinless, and Jesus, not Muhammad, will have a second coming to earth. The concepts of Jesus in the Koran and other Islamic sources invariably have a Divine dimension to them. Muslims do not realize this, in general.

Once saved, my refrain became, "Whosoever denies Me before men, him will I deny also before My Father in Heaven, and whosoever confesses Me before men, him will I also confess before My Father in Heaven."

I was impressed that the Koran stated that there were just two sinless people: Jesus and Mary. I asked, "Isn't it more logical and befitting the majesty of God that Allah should preserve (make sinless) his final prophet, Muhammad?" The Hadith speaks of evil that runs in our bodies, through our blood. But I had not yet a clear idea of original sin.

The story of the annunciation is reported twice in the Koran—3:42 & 19:16–17—but it presumes the knowledge of its readers that Mary was engaged to Joseph the carpenter. Joseph's name, and that he and Mary were engaged, appear nowhere in the Koran.

Islamic commentators on the Koran meticulously examine the engagement between Mary and Joseph. These commentators chiefly relied on the Bible, and so they indirectly admit the reliability of the Bible.

"Mary withdrew to an Eastern place where she stayed behind a curtain ... then We sent to her Our spirit resembling [a] full grown man. She said to him, 'How could that happen, when no mortal has touched me and I am chaste?'"(Koran 19:16–17). Elsewhere, in

Koran 66:12, "and Mary, the daughter of Umran, who guarded her chastity and We breathed into her body Our spirit."

The highly respected Muslim scholar and historian Ibn-Kathir comments and "explains" the previous text when he writes, "We breathed in her through the Angel Gabriel, whom God sent and who resembled to Mary a full man and God commanded him to breathe in her-and This Breath dwelt in her and became Jesus Christ."[103]

I was dismayed and saddened to read that such a scholar could confuse the angel with the Holy Spirit and Jesus, since the angel was a created being, and the Holy Spirit of God was not a created being. The more classic commentators I read, the more I found that agreed with Ibn-Kathir. Even worse, Ibn-Kathir's explanations fit perfectly with the content and implications of the texts in the Koran. THUS I REALIZED THE INCARNATION OF DEITY IN JESUS WAS CONFIRMED IN THE KORAN.

I wondered what shock I would have next! Could it be true that this Jesus Christ could be God Himself? How and why would God go through such a humbling as to come in the form of a man? The implications were *too overwhelming* to comprehend without further study. What came years later was nothing short of the proverbial last straw that broke the camel's back.

WAS HE IN FACT CRUCIFIED?

Islam, unlike any other known faith, vehemently denies the crucifixion. The Koran claims that Jesus only swooned, and He did not die. It claims that Allah replaced Jesus with a look-alike on the cross. In so doing, it completely denies the meaning of the crucifixion, since man has no need of redemption.

Like any other Muslim, when I read that Christians believe that Jesus Christ is the Son of God, and that they imagine that God went to the cross, I could not help but be angry with "the Christians who utter such blasphemy on God." Anger most often blinds the mind, pushing revelation from God to the back burner, squashing the conscience, and making sound judgment impossible. I was for years unwilling to hear the other side, and even worse, unwilling to read any more in an open-minded fashion. It would be years before the Lord refreshed my struggle.

Eventually, I had no choice BUT to look into the Koran and Islamic sources to see whether Jesus was crucified or not. It was these sources that led me to believe that it was Jesus Christ who was crucified and not someone else on the cross in His place.

Koran 4:157 reads,

> And because of their saying: we slew the Messiah, Jesus son of Mary, Allah's messenger. They slew him not, nor they crucified him, but it appeared so unto them; and Lo! Those who disagree concerning it are in doubt thereof; they have no knowledge thereof save conjecture; they slew him not for certain.

I knew that many verses in the Koran were in contradiction to others. I wondered if perhaps Allah had nullified this with other texts. Unanimously, all Islamic scholars deny that Jesus was crucified based on the verse above. But I was unwilling at this point to take the Koran at face value and knew that I must approach the Koran in a broad system of study.

I needed to know who this "someone else" on the cross was, and WHY Jesus was spared. I had to ask if Jesus died at all, or was He assumed into Heaven to return later to earth, and die at a future time, as the Koran states? These may sound amusing to the Western Christian, but they are probing, mind-boggling questions for a seeker who was taught wrongly about Christianity, as a child.

First scenario: Jesus was not crucified, but without death, He ascended alive into Heaven.

The Koran quotes Jesus as an infant, speaking in defense of His mother's reputation. She was questioned by people how she had a child while she was, as yet, unmarried. Jesus, the infant, said, "Peace be upon Me the day I was born, the day I will die and the day I will be resurrected again" (Koran 19:33).

We have Jesus speaking a sequence of events: His birth, death, and resurrection.

The Koran says that Jesus did not die, but was taken up to Heaven alive. But if Jesus was not crucified, who was crucified in His place? So then at what point will He die, as He prophesied in the Koran?

Muslim scholars do not agree who actually died on the cross that was meant for Jesus. Most skirt around it by saying, "a substitute." Some say it was Judas Iscariot, others say it was Peter (Simon), while others speak of Andrew. There is no consensus.

Muslims refer to this as the "Substitution Theory." A substitute is adequate for them.

In Koran 3:55, Allah said to Jesus, "I am about to cause You to die, and I will raise You up to Myself and clear You of those who disbelieve You."

Here is the problem: Some believe Jesus has not died His first death yet, while others interpret this same verse to mean that He did die [other than on the cross] and His grave is in India. Muslims disagree on the meaning of the words "Ini mutawaffika." A majority believe that it means "I will cause You to die," while a minority say that it means to think that God raised up Jesus to Himself alive." But WHY would Allah prevent Jesus from being crucified? In either case, they say that Allah did not want Jesus to go through the shame and ordeal of suffering on the Cross.

It is firm Islamic doctrine that one of the major signs of Judgment Day will be the Second Coming of Jesus Christ. (Shiites believe the Twelfth Imam will appear.) The mission of Jesus' Second Coming has shocking elements for the Christian reader. In Muhammad's Ahadith, "Isa [Jesus Christ] son of Mary will descend on earth, marry and have children and live forty five years and then die and will be buried with me in the same grave."[104] Muhammad states that Jesus in His Second Coming will destroy all the crosses on earth, be a Just Judge for mankind, and Jesus will convert all of humanity to Islam![105]

More shocking claims about the mission of Jesus in His Second Coming come from two of the most reliable "collecting editors" of Muhammad's Tradition, namely Sahih Muslim and Sahih Bukhari, who report another mission Jesus will carry out is killing the anti Christ! Lo! We finally have another prophet besides Muhammad who sanctions killing!

Problems with the first scenario: According to the Koran 19:33, Jesus is still alive. But Muhammad says that when He comes again, ON Judgment Day, Jesus will live for many years, marry, and die. But ON Judgment Day, there is no more death. All people are resurrected, and face either eternal fire in hell or eternal life in Paradise.

For both verses to be fulfilled, Jesus would need to have a Third Coming ON Judgment Day, because He will marry, live for 45 years, etc., and this would take time upon His Second Coming. If we assert He has only one more time to come, and that He has not died on the cross, then we have *one birth, one death, and no resurrection.*

The second scenario: If Allah did cause Jesus to die (other than on the cross) and took Him into Heaven, but He returns to marry, have children, kill the anti-Christ, and die, then we have *two lives, two deaths and two resurrections.* The people who believe that He died also believe that he will come on Judgment Day, kill the anti-Christ, and THEN DIE, to be resurrected one more time. This is extremely problematic, because it would mean He had one birth, two lives, two deaths, and two resurrections. Jesus blessed the DAY He was born, the DAY He would die, and the DAY He would resurrect again.

Implications of the two scenarios: If Muhammad is the final prophet who brought the final and perfect revelation, the Koran, which superceded and abrogated all previous revelations, and Muhammad is the example for all mankind to follow, why is it 1) there is no anti-Muhammad? And, why is it 2) there is a Second Coming of Jesus?

When we analyze the meaning of anti-Christ, we see the ramification is that there will come one who teaches contrary to Christ! If the Koran superceded Jesus Christ's teaching, there is no need for the anti-Christ. It should be an anti-Muhammad. It would be more fitting to have Muhammad return and convert all humanity to Islam, since Muslims believe that he came to all of humanity, while Jesus came only to the Jews.

It might be fitting to Allah, but not to God. This is nothing but mumbo-jumbo theology. It is not fitting to God. As such, Jesus Christ, when He came, came not only as a prophet, a mere mortal man. He came as something far greater than a human being. We ask the Muslim how Jesus could be worthy to judge all of humanity if He were not Divine? How could He judge all of humanity if He came only to the Jews? Furthermore, to judge each and every person's motives and heart requires OMNIPOTENCE, and OMNISCIENCE, which are ONLY qualities of God.

The Koran says of Jesus, "I watched over them while I was among them, but when You took Me up to Yourself, You watched over them." This means that while Jesus was ON EARTH, He watched over all of humanity. When God took Jesus into Heaven, HE watched over humanity. Jesus interchanges positions of authority with God and He shares Divine nature (omniscience). This compels us to conclude that Jesus Christ and the Father are ONE and the same but appear in two different forms, even at the same time. This is called OMNIPRESENCE.

THIS IS A MATTER THAT MUSLIMS MUST CONTEMPLATE AND DECIDE UPON *while* ON THIS EARTH, *because there is no time left to muse over it* ON JUDGMENT DAY.

The Bible says every knee on earth will bow before Him and worship Him.[106] My Muslim friend, you need to call now upon Jesus Christ as your Savior, voluntarily, while you have a choice. On Judgment Day, you will bow before Him and call Him My Lord and My God, but then you will be doomed to hell. Be mindful of Almighty God Who calls you from the pages of the Bible, saying, "Come, let us reason together; though your sins are as scarlet, I will wash them white as snow."[107]

For the Muslim who is yet unconvinced, we have six different answers about the person who is said to have died on the cross in Jesus' place. All six are impossibilities.

Islamic philosopher Al-Razi looked at the theological implications of the Substitution Theory and found one implication worse than the next. He was a brave soul to do this for us. The Assumption Theory is the same, meaning that someone assumed Jesus' position on the cross in His place. Before we discuss in detail the Assumption Theory or Substitution Theory, we have to ask why Allah would "not allow" Jesus to die on the cross.

Muslim apologists say that Allah did not want Jesus to be tortured at the hand of the Jews, so he raised Him up to Himself (either dead or alive, recall). Koran 3:55 speaks of Jesus' being raised up to heaven (alive or dead). The verse is not certain. See also Koran 5:120. Rather than permit Jesus to be disgraced as malefactor, as the Jews intended, He was, on the contrary, honored by Allah as His messenger."[108] The Substitution Theory was devised by Muslim theologians to deal with the Koran's denial of the crucifixion.

Al-Razi reports six problems, or as he calls them "vagueness," that occur when we say that a substitute person who looked like Jesus was crucified and not Jesus Himself. We list at least fifteen we can put forth.

1. If the likeness (shabeeh) of Jesus were cast upon another person, this makes reality, as we know it, capable of being a mirage. This possibility leads to the collapse of the laws of nature. If they collapse, all of Muhammad's words and deeds and what he conveyed as the Koran would not be reliable!

2. It is sophistry that renders everything meaningless, including the Koran:

    a. Doctrinal errors would abound in the Koran.

    b. How could a Just Allah be a source of deception and confusion?

    c. Muslims always say that Allah will do whatever he likes, except he cannot shed doubt upon himself, or contradict his own words.

3. Jesus was capable of many miracles in His lifetime, even raising the dead, and He was strengthened with the Holy Spirit (Koran 5:110). Wasn't He capable of avoiding the cross? And could not the Holy Spirit have rescued Him?

4. If all previous prophets went to their deaths willingly and suffered torture rather than betray God, then why would Jesus have less of an example? Why would Allah make an exception only in the death of Jesus? Why was martyrdom prescribed for all the prophets except Muhammad? Wouldn't it be more fitting if Muhammad were the one that Allah bestowed such honor upon?

5. Muslims do believe that *Muhammad* was persecuted and beaten by the pagans and Jews. This persecution could have

been stopped as well by the same arguments in # 3 above. But Muhammad was not spared. Yet he died a normal death. It seems more fitting that Allah should have raised Muhammad to heaven "alive" rather than Jesus.

6. If Allah raised Jesus to Himself, alive or dead, why would He need to cast the likeness of Jesus on someone else? Wouldn't that make Him a deceiver, who was betraying the trust of the people? And wouldn't that be inflicting pain on someone else who was put in Jesus' place? The Koran states that no one bears or carries the burden, or sin, of another soul. So, why would Allah make an exception for Jesus and place a look-alike on the cross?

7. BEFORE HE WENT TO THE CROSS, Jesus was beaten to disfigurement, whipped and bloodied. His beard was pulled out. He wore a crushing crown of thorns, which caused His head to bleed profusely. The soldiers took his garments, and His hands and feet were nailed with spikes. He was so disfigured that He was almost unrecognizable as a man. Someone else would have had to endure that pain for the Image to fit his face and body.

8. When He was taken down and buried in the tomb by His disciples, they would have been burying someone else, who could not have resurrected and appeared as Jesus to thousands of eyewitnesses over the next 40 days.

9. If Allah cast Jesus' likeness on someone else, he would be guilty of a sin, which is to lead the faithful astray. Well, maybe Allah can sin, according to Islam, since he can do whatever he pleases.

10. Some say that Judas Iscariot was the one substituted, but Judas hung himself on a tree, committing suicide, immediately after he betrayed Christ.

11. Respected Muslim scholars have dismissed the Gospel of Barnabas as a forgery. It was written in medieval centuries; some say by Dante. The document is considered to be a forgery. But Islamic apologists often quote from this Gospel, saying that it was written in third century Spanish language. There was no

Spanish language then! There are many historical, geographical and doctrinal errors in the forged document, some an apparent assault on Islam, which was not present in the third century, either.

12. The likeness of Jesus could not have been cast on Peter (Simon). Peter was crucified in Rome, and the event is historically documented. Peter went on after the resurrection to become the head of the Church in Jerusalem, and he authored at least two of the books in the Bible. Accounts of him after the crucifixion appear in the book of Acts and elsewhere.

13. If we discredit what Christians have maintained through oral tradition about the historical fact of the crucifixion, then it will lead to discrediting the oral tradition of all prophets, including Muhammad.

14. Jesus' mother was present when He was crucified, and according to the Koran, she was sinless. How is it she would have been deceived if she were sinless? Jesus was taken down from the cross and buried, and His mother was there as well.

15. If the crucified one lived a while after the ordeal, and he were not Jesus, he would had made that clear. It could not have been one of the disciples, since they all continued to live afterward and went forward to proclaim Christ to the nations beyond Israel. The disciples of Jesus went to their deaths without resistance rather than deny the cross, and that would not happen if they were part of some sinister cover-up and Jesus was not crucified.

ARE GOD AND ALLAH ONE AND THE SAME?

Islam, which means "submission" to Allah, is the name of the religion (Deen) that Muhammad claimed to be of Divine origin, dictated to him by the angel Gabriel. A Muslim is the person who adheres to the mandates of Islam. Although the Koran is written in Arabic, the majority of the Muslims are not Arabs.

Muhammad in no way exemplifies submission, the outward characteristic of a Muslim. His approach was to completely reject all those who refused to *submit to him*, agree with him, and/or remain loyal to him. Once Muhammad left behind the distinction between his words and the words of Allah, he demanded submission, almost as if he had blurred the line between himself and Allah.

Muslims, as we said in an earlier chapter, use the redefined meaning of the word "Muslim." Before Muhammad, it meant anyone who believes in God and submits to the will of God. Muhammad changed the meaning to include a belief in Muhammad as the final prophet of Allah, etc., so that today, it is used only to refer to those who hold fast to the mandates of Islam. In this redefining of the Arabic word, they automatically make all other religious people "non-believers" or infidels.

Muslims believe that God accepts only the religion of Islam. "Whoever requests any religion other than Islam, it will not be accepted from him and at the end he will be among the losers." (See Koran 3:19.) It is the *archetype of intolerance* rather than the expression of a loving God. Allah is the great taskmaster, and his subjects are his slaves. All Muslim relationships between husband and wife reflect this mandate of submission, which is characteristic of slavery. Slavery is a glorious and perfect relationship in Islam.

The final prophet Muhammad came for all nations, and the Muslim must believe this. There will be no prophet(s) after him. (Except Jesus when He comes back.) Although the "belief" in all prophets is mandatory in Islam, a Muslim is not permitted to follow or embrace the path of any of the other prophets.

Muslims conveniently believe that Islam abrogated the authority of the previous revelations. Therefore, from the time of Muhammad until Judgment Day, Islam is the deciding factor that differentiates a believer (Muslim) from an unbeliever (Kafir) or Mushrik (one who associates other Divine being(s) with God), or Dahriya (an atheist).

What does the name Allah mean? Muslims believe that Allah's nature is transcendent, beyond human comprehension. (Jews do not claim knowledge of the meaning of "I AM that I AM" that was revealed to Moses on Mt. Sinai. Yahweh, the Name of God, which Jews never pronounce out of reverence, is mysterious, and, to the Jews, beyond human comprehension.)

ON THE OTHER HAND, the Koran declares that there is a *very close relationship* between man and Allah, and there are NO barriers in this relationship. Allah is closer to man "than his jugular vein" (Koran 50:16).[109] "Wherever you may turn your face, there is the face of Allah" (Koran 2:115). The same Koran declares that "Nothing at all is like him [Allah]" (Koran 42:11), and "Allah, there is no god but he; his are the greatest names" (Koran 20:8).

The 99 names for Allah in the Koran are of extreme importance to Muslims, since his names are reflective of his character and his qualities. But we do not find one name of Allah that is LOVE. Just in case anyone comes up with one they have not written, there is the 100th name, which is an unknown name.

A majority of Muslims' houses are adorned with Allah's 99 holy names. Belief in the unity (singleness) of God is the very first pillar of Islamic faith. Both Christians and Jews believe in one God, the God of Israel. Muslims agree that Jews believe in one God, but they deny this to the Christians.

Muhammad bore false witness about the Christians when he said we worship three gods. Not one Christian in history would have ever told him he worshipped three gods. Yet Christianity is believed to be a polytheistic faith, which is based on the misconceptions in the Koran of the Holy Trinity.

Muhammad failed to accurately portray the Trinity, perhaps because he missed the concept of generation or creation by God. Each species generates its own kind, but only God (through the Holy Spirit's breath) generates both spiritually and physically. Muhammad was unwilling to reverse his wrongly perceived idea of one God in Christianity.

A Muslim DOES NOT BELIEVE that Christians and Muslims worship the same God. They do not think that God and Allah are one and the same, though they will give lip service to this in their efforts to evangelize.

As one reads the Bible and comes to the saving Light of Jesus Christ, he can easily see that God and Allah are NOT the same. However, it seems politically correct to say so. But we must not deny God and make him the same as Allah in the Koran. There is far more that God reveals through Jesus Christ than can ever be contained in the pages of the Koran.

The external and internal integrity of Biblical narratives is self-evident to even those who are not believers. Recorded in the Bible, accounts of history that were thought to be fiction were proven centuries later through archaeology, geology, and other sciences. Even astronomers have proven that there was a miraculous sign in the sky around the time of the birth of Jesus, to name only one.

Is it possible that God and Allah are one and the same? The God of the Bible is the God of Abraham, Isaac and Jacob. He is consistent, unchangeable, a universal Father, and holy. His holiness binds Him to His own Word. He upholds His Word and will not change it. He loves all mankind enough to have sent His only son to die for our sins, and He stands waiting to be reconciled to any sinner who comes to Jesus. He said that there would be no other way than Jesus to eternal life.

Allah in the Koran is inconsistent, changeable, specific to the Muslims, and not universal. He is unknowable and has fathered no one because he has no wife. He is a plotter, which is inconsistent with holiness. He is only interested in the life of the Muslims and wishes the unbelievers to be killed. The God of Israel CANNOT be the same as Allah, who says anything and changes it thereafter to say the opposite.

Is it possible that the God of the Bible, who commands His faithful to pray for their enemies, be the same Allah who calls for the destructions of all one's personal enemies?

Some Christians have been intimidated by the politically correct and secular pressure to say that the God we know is the same as Allah. Muslims love to say we all worship the God of Abraham. Their version of Abraham is not the one we know. Abraham had two sons, but the God of Abraham made it abundantly clear to him that Isaac was the one he was to offer up, and it through Isaac that Promise would be fulfilled.

Muslims believe that the Jews used to be the chosen people, but that they lost this status through faithlessness to God. God made promises to Abraham and gave his descendants land that stretches all the way from Egypt to the Euphrates. This is clear in the book of Genesis.

Muhammad took the status of the chosen people from the Jews, saying that because the Koran was given in Arabic, the Arabs are the chosen people of Allah. God has promised to keep his Covenant, whether the Jews were capable of fulfilling their part of the Covenant or not. The return of the Jews to Israel was one prophecy in Scripture given thousands of years ago. God is faithful and keeps His Promises down through the ages. He is not like man that He should lie or change.

God and Allah cannot be compared, and they are not one and the same. The Muslims who claim so do not say this out of true belief but only to win converts. Otherwise, they would leave Jews and Christians as they are to worship the same God. The very fact that Muslims want to eliminate Jews and Christians proves they themselves do not believe we are following the God of Abraham.

I have a Muslim family by birth, and only God knows how much I care for them and love them. But I know that God's love for them is far greater. I am not going to deny my God, Jesus Christ, for them or any other man. They know I have been saved and have converted to Christianity, and they do not expect me to deny my faith. They are a bit worried I am going to hell, and they wonder why I am not worried I may to go to hell for leaving Islam. But true to Kurdish nature, they also remain open, and every chance I have to witness to them, I use fully.

Before I close this section, I would like to confirm the theological basis for claiming that God and Allah are not one and the same.

Muhammad's understanding of Allah was influenced by the Bedouin culture floating around Arabia during the time he lived (570–632 a.d.).

The first among these influences was the concept of Allah in pagan Arabia; Bedouins had their way of relating to the unknown source of power that dictates day and night, rain and dryness, poverty and richness, etc. In the words of Reverend Joseph Kenny,

> This was heavily occasionalistic and fatalistic, as may have been conditioned by unpredictable rains and consequently unpredictable food supply, and would account for the same trend in the Koran, although modified by emphasis on the free choice of both Allah and man in influencing events.[110]

Occasionalistic and fatalistic Bedouin influences are prevalent in Allah's relationship to his creatures: master to slaves, the Islamic concept of fate, and most importantly, in the limited free will in Islam.

Hence some Islamic schools of philosophy think of creatures as powerless and inactive. Asharite theology teaches that there is no "mother nature" or scientific cause and effect. It is all Allah, acting each moment, to make things happen. Nature, as an active operation, does not exist. God acts directly in every instance on the occasion of the conjunction of what appear to be a cause and an effect.

Other Islamic schools think of human existence as a mirage of existence and that only Allah truly exists. Mary Baker Eddy founded Christian Science on this same theme, saying that only God, who is love, exists. All matter is illusion, and if we could just get the evil thinking out of our minds, we would realize that everything is mind, pure mind, and not matter. This is similar to the Muslims who say that only Allah exists and that human existence is a mirage.

In another sense, the Islamic version of Allah is a pantheistic concept. Just as in Pantheism, the center of the Islamic concept of monotheism (Tawheed) deprives him of being a personal being with whom men can associate. Islam totally rejects any personification of Allah.

If God is in everything and is everything, then there is no distinction between anything, and if everything that exists IS Allah, then that is the same as saying that Allah is *nothing*. It gives us no new knowledge of Allah to say that he is everything.

The truth of the matter is that God has revealed Himself in creation, but He is not the same as His creation. He is transcendent yet concerned about the smallest details in our lives. He is the eternal God who created the universe in less than one trillionth of a second, and who has placed the earth in its exact location so that we could observe and study the universe. Had we been closer to the sun, the brilliance would have prevented us from seeing His glory in the stars. Had we had slightly less atmosphere, we would have been subject to all of the meteors that have crashed on the moon. His creation speaks of His Infinite Glory and His Eternal Wisdom.

He is a very personal God who desires that His children walk and talk with Him, as Adam did originally in the Garden. He gave us free will and risked everything for the sake of love. If He had not given us free will, our love would have been impossible, much like a robot cannot produce love.

The fact that He has revealed Himself through the pages of the Bible is testimony to His desire to be known by us. He does not wish to remain some transcendent "force" that merely created us. He reveals Himself as a loving God, desiring us to have personal relationship with Him through Jesus Christ. He is GOOD, PERFECT, LOVING, WISE, PATIENT, LONG-SUFFERING, GENTLE, KIND, AND HOLY. His Justice and Mercy meet with a kiss in the mystery of the Holy Trinity. Jesus satisfied the requirements of justice on sin, that we might receive mercy.

We can live eternally with this loving Father, who is calling out to every reader through the lines of this book. He speaks in a still, small Voice that does not need to compete with evil. He has conquered Satan, and He reserves a destiny in hell for him at the end of the world, along with all those who freely choose to ignore and deny Christ. The Holy Spirit has been sent to believers, to counsel and encourage us, to lead us to Christ, and to sanctify us holy before the throne of God.

All of these revelations the Muslims consider blasphemy. It cannot be that the richest of all treasures, eternal life through Jesus Christ, can be blasphemy.

Does not the Koran bear some witness to this relationship, when we consider that Allah created Adam to be his agent on the earth? How could

Adam have received the commandment if he did not have communion with Allah? Was it not this communion that was lost by sin? Adam hid from God, and everything of innocence and beauty was lost to him and his descendants when he left the Garden (Koran 2:30).

Muslims will jump up in reaction and say that the commands of the Koran are what we ought to do! It is not about what we can do, but what He did on Calvary.

God made the way back to Him simple. The path of reconciliation is as simple as asking Him to come into your life and receiving the shed Blood of Jesus as payment for your sins. God clothes you with Jesus' righteousness and sees you through His blood thereafter. This was foreshadowed in the animal sacrifices in the Jewish temple, as we said earlier. Their blood was poured on the altar before the Holy of Holies. This was to put the blood between a Holy God and sinful man. The blood of Jesus covers our sins, if we accept His payment for our sins. His righteousness now becomes our righteousness, and we can stand before God without judgment because we are in Christ.

The second source for Muhammad's view of Allah was a Christian sect, the Judea-Christians, also known as Judaizers. They started in Jerusalem and fled to Arabia. Not only did they believe that Jesus Christ was *not Divine* in nature, they held the same belief in the first five books of Moses and the Psalms of David alone.

The third source was the Middle Eastern Christians in Arabia. The Chaldean Church of Iraq originally believed as the Nestorians did; that Jesus was a prophet with one human nature. However, they joined the Catholic Church in the 15th Century, so we must assume their views underwent revision.

The fourth source is the concept of deity among the Arabs of Mecca, Medina and Ta'ef prior to and during the time of Muhammad, called Hanafi. This was the ancient concept of one god.

In the Islamic version of the rosary (Tasbeh), there are 99 beads. Each one corresponds to one of Allah's holy names, none of which is Father. There is no support at all in Islamic theology for using the rosary; it must have come about in imitation of the Catholics. Reciting Allah's names is thought to be a source of grace and strength, and decorating one's house with his names invokes Divine blessings and protections. Among the 99 names of Allah said to be in the Koran, only 73 can be located. 15 others are derivatives from the same name(s) or are verbs like Ghafir (to forgive). Gahfur means "to forgive limited sins," and Ghaffar means to "forgive endlessly." All of these three "names" are from the same verb Ghafara[111] (to forgive).

The last 11 names are outside the Koran, in Muhammad's Ahadith, although the general concepts for these names are present in the Koran. Why are we emphasizing the "names" of Allah, and why are they worthy of our scrutiny?

The names should correspond to a reality that exists, telling us something about the nature of Allah. Suppose I said, "There is something that is called, 'vrghfhsnjsl,' which you can not relate to it at all, since it is only a conjecture in my mind, and does not exist in reality." The Koran says, "Apart from him, you only worship names you have invented for yourself" (Koran 12:40. See also 7:71 and 53:23.).

The New Testament speaks similarly, as it warns Christians about unbelievers who "exchange the truth of God for a lie" (Romans 1:19 NIV). Hence, God is "The Truth."

In the Koran, though, we have two texts that speak of Allah in two different and irreconcilable character traits: 1) Allah is the Best Plotter (or Deceiver), and 2) Allah is the most truthful. There can be found no contradiction in the Names of God in the Bible. Hence we must conclude that God in the Bible and Allah in the Koran *cannot be one and the same*. On this we wholeheartedly agree with the Muslims!

GROWING UP UNDER SADDAM HUSSEIN

Let me first say that Saddam was a Sunni Arab, from the sect that believes they are the ONLY chosen people. In general, there is a prejudice among Arabs against all Sunni Kurds, and all Shiite Muslims, and all non-Sunni Arabs. Their idea of utopia on earth is comprised of only Sunni Muslims who think exactly the same. Bin Laden is a pure example of this thinking, extended through his terrorist life of Jihad. The surrounding countries of Iraq tolerated Saddam because he was, at least, a Sunni Arab who hated the same people they saw as enemies.

As result of Kurdish uprisings in Northern Iraq and the Shiites in the South, Saddam's army callously trampled both the Kurds and the Shiites with colossal military campaigns. In the 1980s, while I was a youth, Saddam destroyed over 4,000 villages. Hundreds of thousands of young boys, men, women and children were slaughtered with chemical weapons and led into the desert for chemical experimentation (not unlike Hitler's grand experiments). The Kurds that could took refuge in Syria, the Soviet Union (which is now Armenia), Iran and Turkey. The Kurds had no outlet to the sea to escape in boats, as the Vietnamese did. They are a landlocked people. The Kurds have only neighboring Muslim countries that hate them just as much.

The Arab Islamic countries knew full well of Saddam's massacres and crimes against humanity. They did nothing in matters of helping refugees. To the best of my knowledge, I have not seen a single Muslim aid worker in my entire life.

To rub salt in our wounds, *none of the countries in the entire world* raised their voices in condemnation. We only heard the United Nations speak out to save Arab Kuwait.

I was one of those who fled on foot in the snow through the mountains of my homeland, to a camp of refugees in Turkey. On the same night of my arrival, I began to work as volunteer for Doctors without Borders. They had set up a field hospital to treat thousands of young and old people who were dying from severe dehydration and other complications from their journeys.

The Turkish were extremely upset at the influx of Kurds from the mountains, as it was still illegal to say you were a Kurd or to speak Kurdish in Turkey. The soldiers were brutal to the refugees, and some died at their hands. Other starving Kurds refused to eat because they were told they would be poisoned. The conditions in the camps were the most extreme imaginable.

Kurdistan has many tributaries of the Tigris and Euphrates Rivers running through it. It is the center of all of the fresh water in the Middle East, and these rivers serve Turkey, Iraq, Syria, and Jordan, into Israel today. How ironic that dehydration would claim so many thousands in such a rich country as Iraq. We did not have the choice to flee along the rivers. We had to flee for our lives through the shortest routes the mountains provided.

It was at least 30 days before any country agreed to provide blankets and relief supplies to the camps. The first C-130 to come with food and blankets from the United States did NOT come from the government. It came from the Christians who watched our plight on TV.

Thankfully, the United States Armed forces and the allies began a safe heaven zone for the Kurds, later to be known as the no-fly zone. We could return to Iraq, at least, to see what was left of our homes, our crops, and begin again in relative safety. But only the strong could endure the hardships of the mountains a second time.

When we came back from the refugee camps, I was situated in a camp run by John Doe, who was then a major. I worked for a few months with him as his translator. I refused to accept any wages for my work, out of sheer gratitude, since, "The American military came here risking their lives for me and my people, and this is the least I could do for them." I told him this was my reason for refusing compensation for my work, a decision I am so thankful for today.

A year later, in January 1993, while having dinner with a Kurdish friend, a blonde American woman arrived who had known and worked with my Kurdish friend in the US for twelve years. He had fled to the US in 1975. She sat down and ate with the women in the kitchen, though he implored her to come and dine with the men.

His busy schedule was one of the reasons why he asked me to show the American lady our land, as a kind of tourist guide. I spoke English, so it was natural for him to assign me the task. I thought she was another brainless journalist with whom I had had many bad experiences.

He told me that she is a good Christian and a friend of the Kurds in United States. Both reasons motivated me to accept his request to take this woman on a tour around Kurdistan. For the first time, I had a chance to speak to a Christian from outside Iraq!

It had long been a faith I admired, and my curiosity had never been quieted. Finally, I came across someone whom I could ask about Jesus Christ. The other reason to help Sarah was she was, as my friend said, a person who had helped my people for many years in America. We had to be gracious to her.

We were married faster than the blink of an eye. I could say that it was LFFM, which stands for "love from the first moment," and we are more in love now, in Christ, and in the fourteenth year of our marriage. I had asked her to marry me on the fourth day we spent together. That night she had a dream where God told her to marry me.

I was not yet saved, though I told her I did believe that Jesus was the Messiah, and I admonished her to never try to convert me to her faith. She honored this and was silent the first two years. But her silent witness showed me Jesus day by day.

NEW COUNTRY, NEW LIFE AND NEW FAITH

Arriving at Dulles International Airport with my wife, in March, 1993, I could not help but remember what years back my idol, Dr. Martin Luther King, Jr. had said: "Free at last, free at last. Thank God Almighty, I'm free at last." Interestingly, Sara's favorite American was Dr. Martin Luther King, Jr., as well.

I did not realize that he was referring to more than just physical liberty, but he was pointing to the expansive, fresh air of freedom the believer has in Christ Jesus!

So many of the heroes of the Christian faith died, shedding their blood, so that she and I could walk on this land in freedom. So many of its young men and women military heroes have served the country and given their ultimate to keep the land safe through the centuries. I cannot describe the awesome difference I felt in the spiritual atmosphere of the US, as compared to the heinous rule of Saddam in Iraq.

Freedom in the history of mankind never came about without blood. Earthly and spiritual freedom both came as result of blood sacrifice. The former is finite in its scope, while the latter is the real and infinite freedom. And Jesus' blood bought it all for us.

Sara's and my beloved heroes are those precious US military men and women that go around the world, willingly paying the ultimate price, for this freedom to come to those still in bondage everywhere. I thank God for their sacrifices for Iraq every day.

I arrived in America with not such perfect health. Years of jail and torture in Iraq had their toll on my health and my adjustment in America. The most urgent health issue was my teeth. We could not afford health insurance at the time, and certainly not health insurance that covered dental issues.

My wife knew a good Christian dentist who did not mind treating Christians, and anyone who did not have the means, for no return or for very minimal cost. Retired Marine Captain Dr. Luke Blevins was then at least 80 years old. Yet he was as strong as a buffalo and gentle as His Lord Jesus Christ.

My wife told me that she used to go to the same church as Doc Blevins; Christian Assembly, in Vienna, Virginia. She was actually baptized there in 1981. He was a witness to her baptism.

My wife did not speak about Jesus with me because when we were in Kurdistan, she asked me whether I knew who Jesus was. I said I knew He was the Messiah, but I did not want to be forced to convert. I asked her then, "Please never speak about Jesus with me! I know who He is, but I do not want you to influence my decision. If I convert to anything, I will convert to Judaism!"

She honored my request, never speaking about Jesus with me. She just lived as Christ with me. No matter how many tantrums I threw in frustration, and no matter how many times I wanted to walk out on her and spewed out my irritation, she was gentle and kind, and most of all, always forgiving. I suffered from torture and never had learned to live close to another person, especially in a marriage setting.

In Iraq, we do not have girlfriends and dating, so everything was new and uncomfortable for me, and very, very strange. I lashed out at her, blaming her for all my discomfort, but she never yielded to my foolishness, even when I remotely mocked Christianity. Inwardly, Satan was battling to confuse me and keep me from the very Savior for whom I had *yearned* so long.

Sitting down for my first dental appointment with Doc Blevins in his office, he said, "Sir, do you mind if we pray together first?" I shed a few tears upon hearing his request. He was bold in his faith and firmly gentle in his approach. We prayed together, then for the first time. When my wife came back at the end of the appointment, she saw my tears and asked, "Did he hurt you?" I choked up and told her he had prayed with me, and that he was the first person to ever ask me if he could do so.

For the next two years I went back and forth to his clinic to extract my teeth one by one.

During one of these visits, he asked me to visit his church in Vienna, Virginia, near where we lived. During the same visit, while he was injecting Novocain into me, I moved, and the needle landed right in my saliva gland. Within 24 hours, I was unable to work and came home from selling roses during rush hour on Friday; the very hours that we made our profit for the entire week. My wife knew I was really ill to have come home at such a crucial time.

By the next morning, Saturday, I was walking with difficulty. My wife knew that I needed to see a doctor immediately, and we left right then. Fortunately, the doctor had Saturday morning hours. He took one look at me, threw his hands up and said I had to go to the emergency room. I had become so infected that all of the doctors in the small emergency room (perhaps only five doctors) rushed to my side and wheeled me within moments into the operating room. They took X-rays in record time and had me under the knife within 30 minutes.

This clamor left my wife to fill out the forms and literally tell them my name, etc. She was told after the operation that I would be in the intensive care unit for about eight hours, and then I would be transferred to a room. But I remained in the intensive care for eight days! The doctors, we learned later, had not found a single antibiotic that could kill the infection. They were very concerned I might die.

Finally, the last one on their list, which was used on horses, began to work. Later we learned how close to death I had lain over those eight days in ICU.

I was truly alone, in a strange country, with my family 6,000 miles away. There were so many tubes down my throat for eight days, I could not speak, and I was on oxygen as well. No one visited me but my wife. I was afraid to die so alone.

My wife called Doc Blevins during this time and told him what she had learned: that my salivary gland had been removed. He rushed to see me and to pray with me, bringing me a Bible. His visit reminded me of the words of Jesus: "When I was hungry, you fed Me. I was thirsty and you gave Me drink."

With tubes going through my nose, mouth and side, some down my throat, Doc said, "Daniel, how are you doing?" I gave him the high thumbs up. He said, "I want you to know that I will cover all of your medical expenses." I could not answer. Days after that, he visited me again when I was out of the emergency room.

I knew he would come; I knew in my spirit what he would bring with him. He said, "I brought you something you probably will love to read. I brought you the Word of God, the Holy Bible." I extended my hand to receive the book, trying to kiss it, and lay it on my heart. But he did not have a chance to pray the sinners' prayer with me, since the nurses interrupted him, asking him to leave while they gave me some pain medication.

But the Lord hears the prayers even before we can speak them.

The Lord I wanted so desperately was finally drawing closer than ever. It took me, or actually it took the Holy Spirit, over twenty years of intense research and study of both Christianity and Islam to convict this proud soul and bring him to his knees, crying out to Jesus, "Lord, I am a sinner, and I believe that You are the only Son of the Eternal Father. I believe, Lord, You came down from heaven for me and all humanity, and that You went to the cross to be crucified. By Your holy blood, You wash me of my sins. Nothing I do, or am capable of doing will merit a single drop of Your precious blood, but it is the merit of Your blood through which alone I am saved. Lord, I believe that You were born of the Virgin Mary, from Eternity. You are present with God, the Father, since Eternity, and You have risen from the dead by the power of the Holy Spirit through whom You have chosen me and through whose breath I am breathing. Receive me, O precious Savior, in the palm of Your hand, and wash me, oh sweet Jesus, with Your blood, that the death I earned by my sins may pass over me."

Shortly after the Lord healed me that summer day on September 17, 1995, in my water Baptism, I uttered the prayers above. I record them here in my journey towards Christ for all Muslims to read, to contemplate, and to use as a form of surrendering themselves to the loving hand of Jesus Christ, Lord and Savior, now and forever more.

Coming out of the hospital weak and $ 25,000 in debt, I had the greatest treasure of all about to come my way. It was the salvation of Jesus Christ.

I could not accept Dr. Blevins's offer to pay my medical bills. Instead, the Lord Jesus worked yet another miracle, as the hospital forgave us, saying we did not have to pay the bill due to our financial inability. The hand of Jesus was orchestrating the events of my life with clear signs that I could not miss nor credit to any other than Him.

Now I faced the fact that my marriage was going nowhere. We were always in some sort of strife. The worst part was my wife's constant forgiveness of my ever-increasing foolishness. I could not understand how, or why, she kept forgiving me.

I expected punishment due to my sins, but I received mercy and I received forgiveness. My pride and my preconceptions would not allow me to be on the receiving end of a grace I had not earned and did not deserve. This was breaking my pride more and more.

Just as in our relationship with the Lord Jesus Christ, it is not a matter of whether we deserve it or not. No sinner deserves anything other than death. The Lamb of God has provided for our reconciliation, and He loved us before we could love Him. His precious blood merits all we have to give in response; our very heart and mind and soul.

In my marriage, I was unwilling to raise the white flag. I had my childish pride, and I was arrogant. I do believe in raising a white flag and calling a truce. But I had decided within myself that I would be walking away from this marriage.

The Major for whom I had translated in Iraq had become a friend; he lived in Pennsylvania, and he promised that he would find a job for me if I wanted one. Oh, how this seemed to solve every problem I imagined I had!

I was driving to Pennsylvania but found myself in Annapolis, Maryland. As all men, I hate shopping malls. I despise going to women's clothing sections because I have no business there.

My wife had left our marriage to the Lord, since He had told her to marry me in the first place. She was ready to accept His working in me, without co-managing His path for me. She had gone off to work somewhere, unbeknownst to me, in the countryside in Northern Virginia, selling roses that day.

At once I heard a loud, audible Voice telling me, "Go to such a store in the mall, and buy a certain beautiful red dress, and take it to your wife who is at such a place in the country. Tell her that you are sorry, and ask her how to be baptized."

I knew my wife would not believe me, but I really did not care; the voice was so authoritative and strong that I did not dare to ignore doing exactly as He commanded me to do.

FROM ISLAM TO THE FLOCK OF JESUS CHRIST

In late August, we set an appointment with the Pastor to see him and talk about a time for water baptism. I attended the church for a while before September 17, 1995, the day set for the baptism at Christian Assembly in Vienna, Virginia.

This same Pastor, in the same Church, had baptized my wife 14 years before. Before September, I could not help it: just as a back-up plan (in case I died in an accident or from a natural cause), I went ahead and baptized myself. I poured water over my own head while I was alone. I do not remember ever telling my wife about it. It was between God and me.

Now the overwhelming reality of the blood of Jesus started to sink in. I, a sinner, undeservingly received the Son of the eternal Father, who carried my sin to the cross, reconciling me to God.

The moment I stepped out of the water at my public baptism, everything in the world looked and felt new. The Bible, which I had read for so many years, was no more an historical piece of moral literature. It came to life.

Most of what I thought were doctrinal problems were solved without my ever reading a book about the matter. I had access to God and to the Son, and to the Holy Spirit.

Jesus came alive, not as He existed in history 2,000 years ago, but as life-giving Power.

He literally dwelt in my heart, and not transcendent, far beyond the heavens. He was now someone I could talk to. I could speak to Him in my heart, ask Him as many questions as I wanted to, and I would invariably have the answer. He never skirted around the questions but gave life-giving, life-changing answers.

The overwhelming sense of awe of His sacrifice, of His love, of His example has remained an awesome daily expression of the love of the Father. My wife and I still marvel out loud to ourselves the fact that He gave us one another. We no longer fought or had a marriage with strife. For the last eleven years of our married life, it has been a walk of peace, and a walk of trusting Him, no matter what our circumstances. She and I are closer than we ever thought we would be, and yet there are spaces in our togetherness for the Lord. He is first for each of us, and we truly feel we are walking in His Kingdom.

Immediately, as I emerged from the waters of baptism, I rushed to tell the Muslims I knew just what the Lord had done in me. I spent days full of hours of talk back and forth with them, in an Islamic bookstore in Arlington. Their only reaction, hours later, to all of the joy I felt, was to smile at me and say, "That's nice." I finally realized they were close-minded, as I had been for so many years, and that their time had not come. I had planted as many seeds as I could, knowing as little as I did from the Bible.

I determined to study and memorize as much as I could from the Bible. God had neatly organized our business so that I had eight or more hours a day to sell roses with long gaps between customers, where I could study the Word every day, all day long. I soon began to realize that He had given me the heart and the gift for evangelism. My wife became jealous because I was winning souls right and left. But this was a heavenly jealousy. It spurred her to pick up her Bible and read for long hours each day as she sold roses in her own locations. Both of us grew in joy and in the Lord.

She told me that Americans would listen to me because I had a foreign accent. I could get their attention, and they would think it "cute" that I, a foreigner, had come to Christ. I used this to my full advantage and witnessed to every single customer as I wrapped his roses. I laid books by my side, to pique their curiosity, such as "Liberalism Is a Sin." The customer would ask about it, and BAM! I began to talk about sin, not liberalism. I found hilarious and joyful ways to pull each different personality type into a brief encounter with Christ.

I recall one day, the radio in my car at work was playing a Gospel song. A customer waiting asked me to turn it down, and I told him I would not.

He said he would walk away if I did not turn it down, and I said, "Well, then, just buzz off." I was taking a stand right and left for my Lord, who had waited patiently for 36 years, saved me from at least three of Saddam's death sentences, saved my marriage, and given me life more abundant. I was brimming with joy and having a lot of fun doing the most menial of jobs: selling roses from my car by the side of the road for $5.00 a dozen.

Needless to say, living in the Washington, DC area is expensive. My wife and I both had to work six days, and sometimes seven, on holidays, in winter and summer, all year long, to barely make a living. But we had it ALL. We needed nothing more than to pay our bills and feast at the Lord's Table. The wife that He chose for me loved me through thick and thin and really wanted nothing of material value. We lived like this, drinking in God's Word, for many months.

My customers began to bring their sons or their daughters to me for counseling, if you can imagine that. Backsliders would stop to buy roses, and I had them hooked; I got many to return to their faiths simply because it was the Holy Spirit, using my once-dead mouth, to speak life to them. The Lord gave my Kurdish mind the ability to remember whole verses of Scripture and where they were located, so I had plenty to give these thirsty souls.

Wouldn't you guess that Satan was mad? He found a way we could get rich! We were nearly sidelined with a wonderful new business, with all of the breaks anyone could ask for. But we realized at the very last moment, after having gotten a miraculous financial deal that would not allow us to witness at all. I would have to rush from place to place on an exact schedule, down to the minute, and I literally would not have a spare moment if someone were ready to come to the Lord. No matter how we thought about it, the business depended on my being exactly on time at different locations. We walked away from $3,000 a day, which was huge money for us.

We realized that this could NOT be God's Will, even though our flesh wanted it. We decided that nothing could be right if it did not use our talents and gifts. So we never looked back, and we stayed poor for the coming 9 years. We literally worked each day to pay a particular bill, most only in the amount of $100 or so. It took two of us working in the hot sun all summer, or in the freezing cold all winter, to survive. But we had enough to tithe and enough finances to share with those the Lord put in our path.

I remember the Lord providing for my wife to help some destitute Mexicans without work. I remember we bought groceries for others as well and gave, though we had little. We always had enough to tithe and help others, though we seemed to have nothing by the world's standards. We never questioned what we were doing for a living, though it was humble.

I worked in the same place every day, with all of the legal permits I needed. However, my wife took chances and moved each day, since she sold the roses that needed to be sold on that very day, in volume. My wife prayed regularly for the police to pass by; that she would be invisible to them. Sometimes she would work in spots where the police should have kicked her out or given her a ticket for vending along the side of the road. But invariably, if she prayed, they would pass by, not even turning their heads to look.

And when she got too cocky and forgot to pray, they would catch her. The Lord was dealing with her issues as well as mine, and we loved it.

I went back to the Islamic bookstore and got all of the scholars' writings. I got the Koran in Arabic and English. I studied more fiercely than ever and began to write. I got a computer and taught myself how to use it. I wrote and wrote and wrote about Islam and Christianity. Over the years, I wrote as many as eight books, one of which was published in 2003. There was article after article in which I wrote about different subjects. Much of this material I am working with to organize and publish.

I am continuously mindful of the cross and the beautiful hymn, "Were you there when crucified my Lord? Were you there when they nailed Him to the cross? Oh, oh, sometimes it causes me to tremble, tremble, tremble."

You and I, my dear Muslim friends, WERE there. WE nailed Him to the cross; WE spat on Him; WE mocked Him, and WE crowned Him with thorns. But also, my friends, although we did all of these and continue to do so by sinning against Him, He never changes in His love for us, and He is prompting us to call on Him in our hearts.

Calling on Him in our hearts is just the breaking through the hard-shelled seed that He has planted in the conscience of every man on earth. It sends forth roots below the surface in our experiences in life, which are undeniable miracles He wrought for us. He saved our lives. He said a kind word to us when we needed it, or He offered us mercy when we should have died.

The roots alone cannot survive until they send up a shoot, which breaks forth into the light above and begins to take in the sun. To flourish, the tiny plant must now grow leaves. We must acknowledge Him in public and tell others, as He said, "Whosoever confesses Me before men, him will I also confess before My Father in Heaven. And whosoever will deny Me before men, him will I also deny before My Father in Heaven."[112]

It grieved me that so many in the Middle East have not heard the Gospel once, yet those in the West have heard it over and over again. I cried for them many times, and I asked many pastors I met selling roses if they thought about evangelizing overseas. Finally, I began the work to form the non-profit organization, Christian-Islamic Forum. It was finalized in August, 2001, and my first speaking engagement was scheduled for the evening of September 11, 2001. We all know what happened that day. God Himself spoke; He had allowed it to become abundantly clear the time was getting late. The ugly historical sword of Muhammadanism had arrived, and we in the West woke up to the deadly efforts of fanatical Muslims to evangelize using fear and terrorism. These were the only methods Muhammad ever found successful. Thus, the history of Islam continues a long bloody war on the infidels, even in our modern times.

In terms of all He has done for me, I cannot, and will not, shut my mouth and keep Christ to myself! He did not die for me alone! He told us to "Go and make disciples of all nations, baptizing them in the Name of the Father, and of the Son, and of the Holy Spirit." We cease to be Christians if we keep the faith to ourselves. We cannot be Christians and do nothing! May we find the workers to go out into Muslim lands and if necessary, die for others, for the sake of our Lord, as He died for us. Jesus deserves every soul the Holy Spirit will bring to Him through us; and if not me, then who shall go?

Christianity is not a pacifist faith. It is life-receiving and life-giving! We simply cannot go about our daily affairs while millions of Muslims and billions of others will go to hell without our evangelism. Because we are lazy, ashamed, wishy-washy, politically correct or lukewarm Christians, we will have a rude awakening when we have to account to the Holy One for how we spent our time, our most precious commodity.

Being mindful of this, I began with even more fervor after September 11, 2001, to speak nation-wide about the passion of Christ to all Muslims, encouraging those who listened and those who were interested. Numerous Muslims came to sit in the back rows to hear me speak, thinking they would hear a Muslim preaching Muhammad to the unbelievers!

It certainly was never advertised this way, but the Lord caused them somehow to think whatever brought them in. Some walked out, some stayed and asked questions, and some even began to search and seek the Lord. I WAS HAVING SO MUCH FUN.

I never held my tongue when I saw a church that was rich nearby a church that was poor. I admonished and made full use of the fact that I am a foreigner with an accent. I still get away with a lot because of it, and I do not resist exhorting others as strongly as I can. The days are winding down when we have the light. Soon it will be dark, when no man can work and no man further will be saved. May we all stop worrying about what others think of us, and as iron sharpens iron, let us be faithful to Him who has given everything for us . . . may HE be pleased at what we do with the talents He gave us!

EVANGELISM:
THE CROWNS AT HIS FEET

I was and am, to some extent, still intellectually prideful. My wife helps me with that, and I am sure you husbands out there know what I mean.

My wife had, for many years, believed that she was called to the Kurds in the Middle East. She had been working for them on a volunteer basis since 1980. She lost all of her friends when she came to Iraq in 1993 to discern what God wanted her to do there. They decided she was literally crazy. Even her family thought she had "lost it."

One day, after I had been saved, she mourned for the Kurds and asked the Lord why He had not let her witness to the Kurds in Iraq. Had He forgotten about that? He immediately answered her in her spirit that, "You want to go way over there and witness, while you have not made a single effort to witness to all the neighbors around you?" So she felt convicted, and we began a Bible study for the neighborhood. She wrote and delivered over 600 invitations on foot to all the townhouses around us. We had Baptists, atheists, and other full-Gospel Christians come to the Bible study. We were ready to seek the Lord, regardless of denomination.

In August, 2001, I successfully formed a non-profit organization called Christian-Islamic Forum to establish a dialogue and evangelize Muslims. The first public meeting was set for September 11, 2001, in Annandale, Virginia. Needless to say, on September 11, that meeting was cancelled in lieu of evening religious ceremonies. So many Americans showed up in churches around the nation, but sadly they quickly forgot to continue to draw closer to God.

In 2005, I went to see a special man, the Pastor of Word Alive International Outreach in Oxford, Alabama. What a refreshment that was to my soul!

The Pastor, Kent Maddox, I found to be a man true in words and deeds, and a humble man of God. He evidences a holy love, and a joy for evangelism. My wife and I drove many times to Alabama to drink in the fresh spirit of evangelism through our Lord's own love for the lost. The Sunday gatherings are streamed on the Internet at www.wordalive.org.

The Lord has brought my wife and me through many crises that happened with my family in 2006. I do not need to recount the daily life for those in Baghdad in 2006. But the Savior brought us even deeper joy as He answered our prayers for *a Church after His Own Heart*. Pastor Kent is one man wholly devoted to the Lord, and he is ready to evangelize at every moment. He is a precious saint, a constant witness for my wife and me to the glory of the Lord. He has a genuine heart for the Muslims, and the Lord is showing us where our best talents can be employed.

I learned my lesson well that if you trust in men, men will disappoint you. God will never disappoint you.[113] Ever since, and through His mercy, and forever, I remain in His palm.

My wife now knows that her trip in 1993 to witness to Muslims is coming full circle to fruition. I was one Muslim that the Lord wanted to reach through her obedience. She and I are working together on my other books. The one that succeeds my testimony, *Out of Islam, Free at Last*, is written specifically for women in Islam. It is also for every woman considering marrying a Muslim. I have another book underway that tackles slavery in Islam and the treatment of minorities in Muslim lands. Another one is due on Father Abraham, and still another is ahead on the Kurds and Zoroastrianism. The Lord has much to say through this small servant, and He knows the needs of the Muslims who remain in darkness. I hope to translate the entire Bible one day into my native language, Kurdish. This is an awesome and splendid task, if the Lord so desires to do it through me.

May all my Muslim brothers and sisters, languishing still under Islam, one day be blessed with the gracious Lord and Savior, Jesus Christ. I will live every day to see that this happens. We shall shed our crowns at His feet and cry, "Holy, Holy, Holy, Is The Lamb!" And may this be sung in *all tongues*, by former Buddhists, Hindus, Confucians, Muslims, and yes, even former atheists.

Which of these will you have brought to His Feet?

ENDNOTES

1. *On the Grace of Christ and the Original Sin*, by Saint Augustine. Published online at http://www.ewtn.com/library/PATRISTC/PNI5-6.HTM
2. *Koran* 112
3. *Koran* 30:41
4. *Koran* 76: 21
5. *Koran* 76: 19
6. *Mishkat Al-Messabih*, by Al-Tabrizi, book 2, page 383, Hadith Number 5552. Edited by M. N. Temem and H. N. Temem. Publication of Dar Al-Arqam Bin Al-Arqam. Beirut, Lebanon.
7. *Mishkat Al-Messabih*, by Al-Tabrizi, book 1, page18, Hadith Number 10. Edited by M. N. Temem and H. N. Temem. Publication of Dar Al-Arqam Bin Al-Arqam. Beirut, Lebanon
8. *Koran* 2: 31–33
9. For the creation and fall of Adam, see *Koran* 2:30–38, 15:26–39, 20:115–126, and 38:72–83.
10. *Koran* 7:20–22
11. *Koran* 38:75–76
12. *Koran* 20:120–121
13. *Koran* 2:36
14. *Koran* 2:37

15 *The Meaning of the Holy Koran*, by Abdullah Yusuf Ali. Page 349, note number 1006. Amana Publications, Maryland, USA.

16 *Koran* 20:115

17 *The Meaning of the Holy Koran*, by Abdullah Yusuf Ali. Page 1527. Footnote #5688. By Amana Publications. Maryland, USA.

18 *Koran* 70:19

19 Imam Muslim, *Sahih Muslim*, by Abdul Hamid Siddiqi, trans., Kitab Bhavan, revised edition 2000. Vol. 4, book 31, no. 6409.

20 *Koran* 6:164

21 *Sahih Bukhari*, vol. 6, book 65, Hadith number 4736.

22 *Mishkat Al-Messabih*, vol. 2, nos. 5608–5609.

23 *Sahih Bukhari*, Volume 4, Book 55, Number 552.

24 *The Meaning of the Holy Koran*, by Abdullah Yusuf Ali, Page 26. Footnote # 53. Amana Publications. Maryland USA.

25 *Tarih Al-Tebari*, Volume 1, page 76, publications of Dar El-Kutub Al-Elmeya. Beirut, Lebanon, 1997.

26 *The Heart of Islam, Enduring Values for Humanity*, By Seyyed Hossein Nasr.

Publication of Harper, San Francisco. A division of Harper Collins publishers. Page 15

27 Brochure #3, *Towards Development of Islamic Medical and health Sciences through North American Secular Universities IISTD*/Institute of Islamic Sciences, Technology, and Development.

"Islamization of all knowledge and its use, including medicine and the health sciences, are Islamic duties and pragmatic necessities. Muslims should undertake studies, research, and teaching in Islamic and comparative medicine and health sciences in North American educational and research institutions within their institutional constraints. They have great potential due to their belief in freedom through promotion of diversity, ethnicity, and multi-cultural opportunities.

"The structure of academic programs has flexibility too. The Islamic Medical Association of North America, IMA, and similar specialized associations should promote Islamization, through discipline-oriented institutionalized studies and professional practice. IMA, 950 75th Street, Downers Grove, IL 60516. Tel: 630–852–2122. Fax: 630–435–1429.

E-mail: IMANA@aol.com Website: www.imana.org This must be done in cooperation with the experts in Islamic social and humanistic sciences through inter-disciplinary studies and research, and participation of non-Muslim scholars, students, and professionals."

28 *The Spirit of Islam, Doctrine& Teaching*, by Afif A.Tabbarah, page 384

29 *The Oxford History of Islam*, edited by John L. Esposito, Publications of Oxford University Press, Chapter One: *Muhammad and the Caliphate*, by Fred M.Donner, page 8.

30 *Tarih Al-Tabari*, Volume One, Publication of M.A. Baython, Dar Al-Kutub Al-Ilmeya. Beirut, Lebanon, page 549

31 *The Duty of Da'wah*, by Ama F. Shabazz, from an article published on the Internet at www.messageonline.org/2002junejuly/cover4.htm

32 *Mishkat al-Masâbîh*, by Al-Tabrîzî, edited by Muhammad Nezar Temem & Haythem Nezar Temem (Beirut: Dar Al-Arqam Bin Al-Arqam), First Volume, p. 40, Hadith Number 119.

33 Abu Ala' Al-Mawdawe is one of the most influential Islamic thinkers from Pakistan, whose writings were a source of Islamic revival and had great appeal to the whole Islamic world. He founded the Jamat-I-Islami in Pakistan.

34 *Koran* 10:94

35 Note here that believing in what was revealed to the Jews and Christians is *mandatory* for Muslims, which undermines Muhammad's claim that the Bible was corrupted.

36 Abu Al' Al-Mawdawe, *The Introduction to the Koran*. "This Surah consists of four discourses. The first discourse (vv. 1–32) was probably revealed soon after the Battle of Badr. The second discourse

(vv. 33–63) was revealed in 9 A.H.[nine years after his migration to Medina] on the occasion of the visit of the deputation from the Christians of Najran. The third discourse (vv. 64–120) appears to have been revealed immediately after the first one. The fourth discourse (vv. 121–200) was revealed after the Battle of Uhud."

37 *Tarih Al-Tabare*, first Volume, page 567. Publication of M.A. Baython, Dar Al-Kutub Al-Ilmeya. Beirut, Lebanon

38 *Stories of the Prophets*, by Ibn Kathir. Translated by Sheikh M. M. Gemeiah and Edited by Aelfwine Acelas Mischler. Publication of El-Nour for publication and translation Est. Page 403

39 *The Oxford History of Islam*, edited by John L. Esposito, Publications of Oxford University Press, Chapter One: *Muhammad and the Caliphate*, by Fred M. Donner, page 9

40 Koran 3: 67 "Abraham was neither Jew nor Christian but a Muslim." Islamic commentator on the Koran, Ibn-Kathir in his book, *Tafseer Al-Qora'n Al-Atheem*, Volume one, page 364. Commenting on the previous text of the Koran and reasons for its revelation, he said, "A group of Christians and a few Jewish Rabbis were meeting with Muhammad, and they disputed about Abraham. The Christians said he [Abraham] was a Christian and the Jews said, 'But he was a Jew,' and because of that, the next day Allah revealed to Muhammad, that Abraham was neither a Jew nor Christian, but a true believer and a Muslim." The contextual meaning, therefore, could be that Abraham was a Muslim, in the sense that he submitted to God.

41 Abdullah Y. Ali in *The Meaning of the Holy Koran*, Amana Publications, Maryland, USA. pg.129. Note number 352 states that the number of the Muslims in the battle of Badr was 313, and this was in 624 a.d., two years after Mohammed's migration to Medina.

42 Ibid page 10.

43 Some Muslim scholars offer the explanation for Jesus' great miracles as follows: Each prophet that came before had produced miracles needed to win over the people. The Jews were advanced in medicine, so Jesus produced great miracles of healing which would be suffi-

cient to convert the Jews. However, many Christians and Jews asked Muhammad for miraculous signs that he was a prophet. This added salt to the wounds rejection Muhammad received, as he was unable to produce any compelling evidence that God was with him.

44   Muslims will answer this question by saying thousands in modern day convert to Islam without any force. There has been nothing but blood in its 1500 years of history.

45   The notion that Christians and Jews tampered with, and changed Scripture is a false and unsupportable claim which appears in Islamic theology.

46   This was a Jewish tribe in Medina.

47   This is the first month in the lunar calendar.

48   A.H. Stands for After Higra, the migration of Mohammed in 622 a.d. to Medina, and the first year of the Islamic lunar calendar.

49   Abu-Ala' Al-Mawdawe, *Introductions to the Koran*.

50   *Tarih Al-Tabri, Tarih Al-Omam wa Al-Muluk*, by Al-Tabari, volume two, page 48. Arabic Edition 1997. Publication of Dar Al-Kutub Al-Illmeyya. Beirut, Lebanon.

51   *Introduction to the Holy Koran*, by Abu Ala' Al-Mawdawe.

52   *Introduction to the Holy Koran*, by Abu Ala' Al-Mawdawe.

53   *Koran 42: 13*

54   *Koran 22: 78*

55   *Koran 2: 132*

56   *Sahih Al-Bukhari*, Volume 5. *Hadith* Number 169. Abu Ala' Al-Maududi, in the *Mohammed Encyclopedia of Seerah*, Vol. 4, Book Seven, chapter forty-one, page 570, says..."Abraham, the originator of this prophetic civilization [Islamic civilization], raised its edifice on the foundation of Allah's **Unity.**"

57   *Koran 37:100–101.* Please read the text from Verse 91–103

58   *Koran 11:71–72*

59   *Koran 14:35–39*

60 *Koran* 10:47. See also 16: 36, 35: 24

61 *Koran* 14: 4.

62 *Koran* 45:16. See also *Koran* 44:32–33.

63 "Tribes" here is a reference to the twelve tribes of Israel. Of course, Muslims *do accept* the notion that God was the one who formed these tribes. Jesus, according to Muslim commentators, had 12 apostles, one from each tribe of Israel. Jesus chose the 12, and He was the head of them. Who was Jesus representing here when He was not one of them, but their master, teacher and example?

64 *Koran* 10: 37

65 *Koran* 2: 2

66 The Shiite call of prayers is entirely different at its end than the Sunnis' call of prayers. Shiites do not recognize the first three Caliphs. Shiites believe in "temporary marriage," while Sunnis do not. Shiites believe in venerating the shrines of their Imams. Sunnis theoretically do not believe in the veneration of shrines, but in reality, they practice the same. Shiites believe in the supremacy of their Ayatollahs as valid leaders of the faith; Sunnis are on their own. In a nutshell, Shiites bear resemblance to Catholics in leadership structures, while Sunnis bear resemblance to Protestants, without formal structure.

67 Published online at http://www.catholic.com/library/Papal_Infallibility.asp

68 "This means the turning away of wrath by an offering. It is similar to expiation but expiation does not carry the nuances involving wrath. For the Christian the propitiation was the shed blood of Jesus on the cross. It turned away the wrath of God so that He could pass 'over the sins previously committed' (Romans 3:25). It was the Father who sent the Son to be the propitiation (1 John 4:10 NIV) for all (1 John 2:2 NIV)". www.carm.net/dictionary/dic_p-r.htm

69 *Sahih Muslim*, Vol 4, page 1261, Hadith #5838.

70 *The Religion of Islam*, by Maulana Muhammad Ali. 6th Edition. Printed in the United States by Book Crafters, Chelsea, Michi-

71 *The Religion of Islam*, by Maulana Muhammad Ali. 6th Edition. Printed in the United States by Book Crafters, Chelsea, Michigan, USA. Copyright of the Ahmadiyya Anjuman Isha'at Islam (Lahore). Page 177 and note 24 in page 178.

72 *The Meaning of the Holy Koran*, by Abdullah Yusuf Ali. 10th Edition. Amana Publications. Maryland, USA. Page 789, footnote number 2644.

73 Please see my article titled, "Demystifying Jihad" in *Envoy* magazine, which is available on the Internet.

74 The prophet here is Muhammad.

75 *The Meaning of the Holy Koran*, by Abdullah Yusif Ali, Amana Publications, Maryland. 10th Edition. Appendix II, Page 290.

76 Ibid.. Page 262, Note Number 753.

77 *The Meaning of the Holy Koran*, by Abdullah Yusif Ali, Amana Publications, Maryland. 10th Edition. Page 238, Note number 669.

78 Ibid, Page 292 appendix III

79 *Koran* 42:13

80 "And as for Ishmael, I have heard you: I will surely bless him; I will make him fruitful and will greatly increase his numbers. He will be the father of twelve rulers, and I will make him into a great nation. 21 But my covenant I will establish with Isaac" (Genesis 17:20 NIV).

81 The Koran uses the term "Injil" in reference to the "Gospel of Jesus Christ." By this, they mean a revelation consistent with the Koran. Muslims claim that God revealed to Jesus a book of which we have no copy. (This conveniently allows them to go on and "tell us" what was in that book.) What Christians refer to today as the "Gospel" is not the same "Gospel" as referred to in the Koran.

82 "Now a man named Ananias, together with his wife Sapphira, also sold a piece of property. With his wife's full knowledge he kept back

part of the money for himself, but brought the rest and put it at the apostles' feet. Then Peter said, 'Ananias, how is it that Satan has so filled your heart that you have lied to the Holy Spirit and have kept for yourself some of the money you received for the land? Didn't it belong to you before it was sold? And after it was sold, wasn't the money at your disposal? What made you think of doing such a thing? You have not lied to men but to God.' When Ananias heard this, he fell down and died. And great fear seized all who heard what had happened. Then the young men came forward, wrapped up his body, and carried him out and buried him. 7About three hours later his wife came in, not knowing what had happened. Peter asked her, "Tell me, is this the price you and Ananias got for the land?' 'Yes,' she said, 'that is the price'" (Acts 5:1–8 NIV).

83 "What They Say about the Holy Koran," an article published online at http://www.quran.org.uk/ieb_quran-feedback.htm

84 *The Heart of Islam, Enduring Values for Humanity*, by Seyyed Hossein Nasr. Publication of Harper San Francisco, a division of Harper Collins publishers. Page 20.

85 Dr. Muhammed T. Al-Hilali & Dr. M.M. Khan, *The Noble Koran*, English Translation of the Meanings and Commentary. (Medina: Publication of the King Fahd Complex for the Printing of the Holy Koran,) page 904.

86 Ahadith is the Arabic plural for Hadith, which is commonly known as the words and deeds of Muhammad.

87 *Muhammad Hamidullah, Introduction to Islam, pg 23*

88 "And whatever the Messenger gives you, take it, and whatever he forbids you, leave it. And fear Allah: truly Allah is severe in punishment (*Koran* 59:7).

89 This is from Muhammad's last sermon to his followers before his death.

90 The six articles of Islamic faith are: 1) Shahada (which is the testimony that there is no god but Allah and Muhammad was his prophet.) 2) Belief in the prophets. 3) Belief in the revealed books.

4) Belief in the angels. 5) Belief in the Judgment Day. 6) Belief in Qadar (destiny or fate.)

91 See also *Koran* 2:89

92 *Koran* 29:46

93 *Allah: Is He God?* by P. Newton and M.R. Haqq, 1991. Pioneer Book Company, Page 1.

94 *Koran* 4:46

95 *Koran* 5:13

96 There are six articles of Islamic faith and five pillars. The five pillars of Islamic faith, briefly again, are the belief in Allah or Credo (Shahada), prayers, fasting, pilgrimage, zakat (tithe), and some of the orthodox Muslims add a sixth pillar to the faith, Jihad.

97 *Koran* 2: 98

98 That is, the Koran was revealed from Heaven.

99 "Then we sent to her our Spirit and assumed for her the likeness of a perfect man. She said: How could that happen when no mortal has touched me and I am a chaste" (*Koran* 19:16–17).

100 *Koran* 66:12 When the Spirit dwelt in Mary, and became Jesus that born child is the son, or product of, the Spirit of God. Ibn-Kather comments on Koran 66:12, saying, "We breathed in her, through the angel Gabriel, whom God sent and who resembled to Mary a full man, and God commanded him to breathe in her, and this breathe dwelt in her womb and became Jesus." Page 402, of Ibn-Kather's *Commentary on the Koran*, Volume IV, Publication of Ali Baythony, Dar Al-Kutub Al-Ilmiya, Beirut, Lebanon, 1997.

101 Published online at http://www.neobyzantine.org/orthodoxy/history/nestorian.php

102 *Tarih Al-Tebari*. Volume 1, page 98, publications of Dar El-Kutub Al-Elmeya. Beirut, Lebanon, 1997

103 *Tafsir Ibn-Kathir.* By Ibn-Kathir. Fourth volume. Page 402. Publication of Ali-al-Baythouni. Beirut, Lebanon, 1997. Dar al-Kutb Lil Maliyyen (Publishing House).

104 *Mishkat al-Massabih*, by Al-Tabrizi. Edited by M.N Temem and H.N. Temem. Publication of Dar al-Arqem bin al-Arqem. Volume two. Page 372–73. *Hadith* Number 5508

105 *Mishkat al-Massabih*, by Al-Tabrizi. Edited by M.N Temem and H.N. Temem. Publications of Dar al-Arqem bin al-Arqem. Volume two. Page 372–73. *Hadith* Number 5505–5507.

106 "Myself I have sworn, my mouth has uttered in all integrity a word that will not be revoked: Before me every knee will bow; by me every tongue will swear" (Romans 14:11 NIV).

107 "Come now, let us reason together," says the LORD. "Though your sins are like scarlet, they shall be as white as snow; though they are red as crimson, they shall be like wool" (Isaiah 1:18 NIV).

108 *The Meaning of the Holy Koran*, by Abdullah Yusif Ali. Amana Publications, Maryland. 10th Edition. Note number 664, page 236.

109 *Mohammed, Encyclopedia of Seerah*, Volume IV. By Afzalur Rahman. Foreword by Dr. A. Nasseef and Dr. M. A. Zakibadawi. Sponsored and published by The Muslims schools trust, London. Page 237.

110 Islamic Monotheism, Principles and Consequences. By Rev. Joseph Kenny

111 Other synonymous verbs are samaha, and safah.

112 "Whoever acknowledges me before men, I will also acknowledge him before my Father in heaven. But whoever disowns me before men, I will disown him before my Father in heaven" (Matthew 10:32,33 NIV).

113 "Then you will know that I am the LORD; those who hope in Me will not be disappointed" (Isaiah 49:23 NIV).

TATE PUBLISHING & *Enterprises*

Tate Publishing is committed to excellence in the publishing industry. Our staff of highly trained professionals, including editors, graphic designers, and marketing personnel, work together to produce the very finest books available. The company reflects the philosophy established by the founders, based on Psalms 68:11,

"THE LORD GAVE THE WORD AND GREAT WAS THE COMPANY OF THOSE WHO PUBLISHED IT."

If you would like further information, please call
1.888.361.9473
or visit our website
www.tatepublishing.com

TATE PUBLISHING & *Enterprises*, LLC
127 E. Trade Center Terrace
Mustang, Oklahoma 73064 USA